"I am the living bread which came down from heaven: if any man eat of this bread, he shall live for ever: and the bread that I will give is my flesh, which I will give for the life of the world"
(John 6:51).

SOUL FOOD

Daily Nourishment from Psalm 119

by Marilyn Hickey
with a special section
by Sarah Bowling

SOUL FOOD

Daily Nourishment from Psalm 119
by Marilyn Hickey

© 1998 by Marilyn Hickey Ministries
P.O. Box 17340
Denver, CO 80217

ISBN #1-56441-036-6
Printed in the United States of America

Unless otherwise indicated, all Scripture quotations are taken from the New International Version of the Bible.

Table of Contents

Introduction

You can think of Psalm 119 as powerful "Soul Food" which can be nibbled on whenever you need a little extra energy, fulfillment, or satisfaction. Simply put, it is a nourishing treat: easy to digest and apply to your daily living. Psalm 119 contains answers for challenges, crises, and problems. It provides the tools needed to maintain a constant communion with God.

The Diary of a Young Man

Psalm 119 reads like the diary of a young man who wants to fully know the Lord. It provides a glimpse of the inner life of someone longing to attain understanding of God's Word and, through it, to achieve moral perfection.

Because it is a Psalm designed for personal meditation, I have included in this book a devotional reading for each verse. Visualize the verses as a six-month supply of delicious food for the soul. Consume one a day— read, meditate, and pray over the designated verse. It will take you six months to finish the entire Psalm and, in one year, you will have prayed over Psalm 119 in its entirety two times. I am certain it will energize your spirit and nourish your life! I have also included a chapter by my daughter, Sarah, which will give you valuable information on how to thoroughly mediate on God's Word. See Chapter 23 starting on page 221.

A Spiritual Journey

The psalmist holds the study of the Word as his highest goal. He begins by reading the Word, but this is not enough. Next he seeks knowledge of the Word from earthly teachers, but even this does not satisfy him. These teachers give him knowledge, but he yearns for understanding. His next step is to ask God to teach him about the Word.

Finally, with the Word embedded in his heart, he endeavors to live his life according to the Word. The understanding of the divine Law is his delight.

There is a lovely symmetry in the psalmist's journey: he studies the Word because he loves God and he loves God because His Word is righteous. As the psalmist engraves the Word in his heart, he delights in obeying its commands. As his obedience grows, so does his love for God, and as his love for God grows, so does his obedience. What a breathtaking voyage!

A Love Affair With the Word

The author of Psalm 119 saw the Word of God as his most prized possession, and understanding that Law was his primary life goal. Almost every verse contains one of these eight words which describe Scripture:

Law: from a verb which means to direct, to guide, to aim, to shoot forward. It is the rule of conduct which was revealed to Moses and perfected in Christ.

Testimonies: from a verb meaning to bear witness. The Ark of the Covenant was referred to as a testimony, as were the two tablets of stone and the Tabernacle itself, in which the Ark and the tablets rested.

Precepts: something placed in trust. The Word is a great gift, entrusted to man by a loving God.

Statutes: something engraved or inscribed. The Ten Commandments were engraved in stone, and the Word is to be engraved on our hearts.

Commandments: pronouncements from God, such as His command to Adam about the tree of knowledge, or to Noah about building the ark.

Judgments: from a verb meaning to govern, to judge, or to make decisions.

Word: the Logos—God's revealed will.

Ways: a plain rule of conduct. The grace of God comes to us through Christ our Lord, Who is the *way*, the truth and the life.

Psalm 119 is "soul food" rich in nutrition that is necessary for growth in God. Take time to savor God's "recipes" for spiritual health. Unlike other food, soul food is easy to digest and the only heartburn it causes is a burning zeal to share it. However, there are two areas where we must be cautious. Many Christians fall into one of two categories in their use of the Word.

Some people are spiritual anorexics. They perceive themselves "fat" in God when they are actually starving their spirits. They don't get enough of the Word, and they tend to avoid other Christians because they don't want others to know they are weak in the Word. These anorexic believers need to get the life and cleansing that only comes from time spent meditating upon the Word. As they do, God will give them His image, and their spirits will grow fat.

Bulimic Christians are binge eaters. They enjoy meals in the Word—church services, tapes, etc.—but they do not apply the Word in their lives. They need to allow the Word to settle into their hearts, and need to change their lives by obeying it. Otherwise, they will not get the spiritual nourishment required for victorious living.

By sticking to a soul food diet rich in prayer and meditation on the Word, you will enjoy all the benefits of a healthy Christian life. Bon appetit!

The Hebrew Alphabet

The Alphabet of Divine Love

The organization of Psalm 119 is a spiritual diagram of our life journey. Some have called it the "alphabet of divine love," because it is based on the Hebrew alphabet. There are 22 letters in the Hebrew alphabet, and Psalm 119 contains 22 corresponding sections, each consisting of eight verses. In each section, the first word of every verse starts with the same letter of the alphabet. This means that there are eight verses starting with the first letter of the alphabet, eight verses starting with the second letter, and so on.

Letters of the Hebrew Alphabet and Their Meanings

The Hebrew alphabet is not a picture alphabet, but each letter suggests a symbol or theme, and each is explained in its own chapter in this book. There is an extraordinary characteristic of the Hebrew alphabet: together the 22 letters describe the character of the Messiah.

Hebrew Letter	Meaning	Application to the Messiah
aleph	the ox (a beast of burden and a sacrificial animal)	He is the servant and the sacrifice.
beth	the house	Jesus Himself is the house of the Lord.
gimel	the burden bearer	He came to bear our burdens.
daleth	the open door	He is our door to salvation.
he	the window	He is our window to God.
waw	nail (literally "and")	He was nailed to the Cross.
zayin	sword of the Lord	He was pierced by the sword; He is the sword of the Spirit.
keth, cheth	enclosed, fenced area	He is the shepherd who guides us into the safe enclosure.

teth	the serpent	As Moses lifted up the serpent, so must the Son of Man be lifted up.
jod, yod, yodh	the open hand	He rules creation. He opened His hands on the Cross to defeat death.
kaph	palm of the hand	He holds us in His cupped hands.
lamed, lamedh	ox goad	He corrects us to get us going in the right direction
mem	water or fountain	He is the fountain of light and life.
nun	the fish	He is a fisher of men. The fish was the secret symbol of the early Church.
samech, samekh	prop or staff	He is our support and our staff.
ayin	the eye	His eye is always on us; the eye is the window to the soul.
pe	the mouth	He speaks the truth. He is the living Word.
tzaddi, tsade	a fishhook; bent in humility	He fishes for our souls; He lived and taught in humility.
qoph	nape; back of the head	He is the head and we are the body.
resh	the first	He is firstborn, firstfruits, beginning and end, the cornerstone, the supreme ruler.
shin, sin	the tooth or to digest	Through Him, we are able to digest the Word more easily; His words had "bite."
tau	a cross-shaped mark or sign	He was crucified upon the Cross; He marks the believers; the Cross is the symbol of the Church.

CHAPTER ONE
Aleph (verses 1-8)

Aleph, the Ox
(pronounced "ah-leff")

Hebrew scholars attribute the qualities of strength and abundance to this letter. Oxen are big and strong, but they are also gentle and hard-working, and always ready for service. The best, unblemished oxen were also used by the Israelites as blood sacrifices.

Several times, the Bible mentions oxen serving as laborers, and then being sacrificed. In I Kings 19:19-21, Elijah found Elisha plowing with twelve oxen. When Elisha decided to follow Elijah, he butchered the oxen, and served them as a farewell dinner to his family. In II Samuel 6, oxen were used to pull the cart carrying the Ark of the Covenant. When the Ark arrived safely, oxen were sacrificed, and a huge celebration began.

In Jesus' own life, there is a beautiful parallel to the qualities of aleph, the ox. As a youth, Jesus grew strong, preparing for a life of service to mankind. That gentle life of hard and heart-breaking work ended, of course, in the ultimate blood sacrifice.

Psalm 119
Verses 1-8

[1]Blessed are they whose ways are blameless,
who walk according to the law of the LORD.
[2]Blessed are they who keep his statutes
and seek him with all their heart.
[3]They do nothing wrong;
they walk in his ways.
[4]You have laid down precepts
that are to be fully obeyed.
[5]Oh, that my ways were steadfast
in obeying your decrees!
[6]Then I would not be put to shame
when I consider all your commands.
[7]I will praise you with an upright heart
as I learn your righteous laws.
[8]I will obey your decrees;
do not utterly forsake me.

Walk in God's Blessings

The Psalmist's Heart: Obeying God's Statutes

The very first word in this psalm is *Blessed,* and the first eight verses describe the glorious state of blessedness for those who walk in God's Word and keep His testimonies. There are two blessings here: an outward one and an inward one. If we keep God's Word within us, God will protect and keep us safe.

The psalmist presents his resolutions to follow God's statutes. He lays these resolutions before the Lord like a sacrifice upon the altar. The psalmist calls to heaven for the fire of God's love to fall upon his sacrifice.

These first eight verses of Psalm 119 portray a man hearing God's sweet, quiet voice whispering behind him the right paths to take. These verses tell us the way our heart is to walk.

This section of the psalm describes a descent from the mount of blessing. It begins with the victorious cries of the obedient in the first verse, and in the eighth verse becomes almost a wailing plea to God.

Don't be depressed—the psalmist wasn't! This is a perfect tale of spiritual growth: going from admiration of goodness to a burning longing after God; from the realization that no man will ever reach perfection on his own, to an intense horror lest God should turn His back. The final joy comes in the knowledge that God will never abandon His believers.

Notice that in verse 8, the psalmist begs God not to "utterly" forsake him. He knows that there is a difference between partial and total desertion. God said He would not forsake His people in I Samuel 12:22. Elijah was forsaken, but not like Ahab. Peter was forsaken, but not like Judas, who was utterly forsaken. David was forsaken to be humbled and bettered, but Saul was utterly forsaken to be destroyed. The psalmist knows that, because he obeys God's decrees, he will not ever be *utterly* forsaken.

Your Walk in the Word: The Path of Prayer

The first verse connects your whole heart with God. Verse 2 instructs you to seek God not just with the cold searches of your brain, but with the deepest longing of your heart. You don't *comprehend* Him by *reason*; you *apprehend* Him by *affection*.

In verses 3 and 4, you can see the perfection of one who walks in His ways. Believers long to be that perfect, but verses 5 and 6 remind you that no one can be entirely perfect, no matter how much perfection is desired. Verses 5 and 6 are prayers to God for help. You simply cannot walk and keep His Word, or keep His statutes unless you pray.

Verse 7 goes from prayer to praise. That's not a long or difficult journey. If you pray for holiness, you will ultimately give praise for happiness.

The Word is a mirror which reflects light for us to walk in, rather than mirroring defeat.

Your Walk in the World: Perfectionism and Fear

There are two traps the world sets for you which the psalmist wrestles with in the first eight verses. The first is perfectionism. Too many people think that they must be perfect in order to be valuable or to be loved. Remember that perfection can only be found in and with God. Your human responsibility is to choose to walk with Him, to read His Word, to observe His precepts, and to learn from the experiences He uses to teach you. This is the only sure path to perfection. You cannot attain perfection by tensing up and trying harder. You can only do it by promise and through prayer. You must seek the Lord with your whole heart, as this psalmist does, and only in this way will you assure your continued growth and blessedness.

The second trap is fear. If you make a bold confession of faith in your private talks with God, but don't share that confession with other people, it may be because you are afraid those people will laugh at you or think less of you. In the keeping of God's statutes, there is a lack of shame. When you respect God, you respect yourself, and then you become respected, in that order. God will protect those who love Him from ridicule and shame. Face the world with confidence! If God is with you, who can be against you?

His Gift for You: Mercy

Isn't it wonderful to know that God will never utterly forsake you? The psalmist here assures you that those who obey God's Law will have God's help. Christians know that obeying God's Law perfectly is impossible without Jesus. Through His blood sacrifice, He has made you righteous and assured you of God's blessing forever.

Dear Lord,
I thank You for Your great and infinite mercy. When I get frustrated with my own failings, remind me to turn to You. Help me to remember that I can grow and learn only through You. When life presents me with trials and challenges, through Your grace, they will only make me stronger. I know that no matter how dark things look, You will never utterly forsake me. Thank You that through Your precious Son's ultimate sacrifice, I will enjoy Your blessings for all eternity.

Amen

DEVOTIONS

ALEPH
the Ox
MEDITATIONS

Day 1

Blessings for the Blameless

¹ Blessed are they whose ways are blameless,
who walk according to the Law of the LORD.

The Law of the Lord is the Law revealed by Moses and perfected by Christ. Reason and logic clearly show that the Law given to Moses by God is the right way to live happy and righteous lives. Isn't it amazing how difficult it can be to follow those laws perfectly? None of us, not one, can claim completely blameless ways. How marvelous that Jesus paid the price of our mistakes, and gave us a new life—a clean slate!

You can't live a blameless life through your own efforts or will power. The only way to grow more and more like Jesus is to immerse yourself in His Word—to seek fellowship with Him with all your heart and soul. The great blessing that Christ gave you is that you are blameless through His Word, and through your delight in His Word.

For Christians, "walking according to the Law of the Lord" is walking in the footsteps of Jesus. It is through His truth, His spirit, and His grace that you are blessed. Oh, what blessings are in store for those who walk in the path that He prepared!

Lord, thank You for preparing the path for me.

Day 2

Blessings for the Seekers

² Blessed are they who keep his statutes
and seek him with all their heart.

Statutes are formal laws. When you love Jesus, you follow His statutes as if they were engraved or written in your heart. They lead to God's own presence. Every one of God's commands leads you away from this world and its sin, and into the holy hiding place where He lives. The strength to follow them comes out of your love and praise for Him, not from any strength of your own.

You can seek God only with your heart. You can't find Him with your eyes; you can't find Him with logic, reason, or science. Only the heart can find God. Only the light from His Word can lead you to Him. You must seek Him with your whole heart, for half-hearted searches will never succeed. When you seek with all your heart, you will find special encouragement to pray.

All through Psalm 119, you will find that praise and prayer always go with learning. Over and over, as you pray, God will teach you to have a praising heart. He will open your heart to receive His statutes, to love His statutes, and to keep His statutes for the simple reason that you want to keep them.

Lord, teach me the joy of a praising heart.

Day 3

Blessings for the God-centered

³ They do nothing wrong; they walk in his ways.

Can you honestly say that you have done nothing wrong? That you will do nothing wrong today? Or tomorrow? The temptations of the world abound. Only through prayer can you escape those temptations and come to a place where following God's Law makes you joyful. When you give your heart and your life to God, He will live in and through you. Then, you will have no desire to rebel. In fact, rebelling will make you so unhappy that you will rush to obey!

Only God can fill your heart with such obedience. If you spend little time in prayer, it is because you are self-centered. Choose today to become God-centered. Spend more time in His Word and in conversation with Him. Ask Him to come into your heart and to fill it. Ask Him for an obedient spirit, and then listen quietly for the answer.

When you are truly walking in God's ways, your flesh will no longer control your actions. It is then that God can truly bless you, answering your deepest longings, because you will long only for those things that are in God's will.

Lord, give me a desire to spend time with You and to listen to You.

Day 4

Blessings for the Obedient

⁴ You have laid down precepts that are to be fully obeyed.

Sometimes you may forget Who set down the precepts by which you are meant to live. Your parents did not create these rules. Your pastor did not invent them. These are the precepts of the Lord! He expects you to not only to follow these rules, but to obey them *fully*. Like a good parent, God expects obedience without hesitation or proffered excuses.

God has trusted us with His sacred laws—His precepts. *Obeying* them is the responsibility of man. When you tell a small child not to run into the street or to stay away from a hot stove, are you instructing the child because it makes you feel powerful? Of course not! You give these instructions for the good of the child. In the same way, God has laid down His laws out of His love for you.

When you find yourself making excuses, pushing God's boundaries, or trying to justify behavior that you know violates God's Law, run to Him in prayer for a reminder that His laws are for your own good.

Lord, cleanse my heart of disobedience.
I want to fully obey Your precepts.

Day 5

Blessings for the Guilty

⁵ Oh, that my ways were steadfast in obeying your decrees!

Have you ever longed for something that was impossible? Here the psalmist expresses a deep longing to perfectly obey all of God's decrees. He is not satisfied just to be happy, safe, or healthy—he yearns to be holy. What a noble aspiration!

Of course, perfect obedience is impossible to accomplish by yourself. The apostle Paul describes this frustration in Romans 7:15, *"I do not understand what I do. For what I want to do I do not do, but what I hate I do."* The psalmist would agree completely with Paul. He longs to obey God, but that is an impossible dream without Christ's gift of grace.

Have you done something wrong? How did you feel? Were you ashamed? Did you want to hide your misbehavior from everyone, even God? When you are feeling guilty, God is the very first One you should seek. In His arms you will find forgiveness, mercy, and the strength to try again. God loves your desire to be steadfast, and He will give you the grace to attain it.

Lord, I want to be Your servant.
Please fill me with the spirit of obedience.

Day 6

Blessings for the Imperfect

⁶ Then I would not be put to shame
when I consider all your commands.

You can have perfect confidence to face the world when you obey all of God's commands. When you obey all of God's commands, you can hold your head high, with no shame, guilt, or embarrassment.

Notice that the psalmist considers *all* God's commands. This is not partial obedience. King Saul killed all the Amalekites but one, and that one exception lost him his throne, and brought him under the displeasure of God. You don't pick and choose commandments. You must commit to *all* of them.

Is your obedience perfect? Of course not! None of us ever has or ever will perfectly obey God's commands—not a single one. *"As it is written: 'There is no one righteous, not even one…' "* (Romans 3:10). That is why we must wrap ourselves in the righteousness of Christ. Christ put to rest our human shame and washed us clean.

As a Christian, you can hold your head high, and not be put to shame.
Lord, thank You for the great price You paid to remove my shame.

Day 7

Blessings for an Upright Heart

⁷I will praise you with an upright heart
as I learn your righteous laws.

There are two "I wills"—one in this verse and one in verse 8. Here, the psalmist has the best of intentions. He wants to follow God's Word with his whole heart. He admits he doesn't yet know all there is to know about God, but he commits to a lifelong learning experience.

Hand-in-hand with learning is praising. When you turn your heart to praise God, you become motivated to learn more about Him. At the same time, the more you learn about Him, the more you are compelled to praise Him! This wonderful, unending circle will improve your heart, your mind, and your life.

Notice that your praise cannot be halfhearted. You must praise Him with an upright heart. This means your praise will be sincere, and it will be for Him alone. You may love your church and your pastor, but your praise is to be for God alone. You may adore your family, but your heart must always be directed to God.

Lord, as I praise You with all my heart,
guide my quest to learn from Your Word.

Day 8

Blessings for the Humble

8 I will obey your decrees; do not utterly forsake me.

The young psalmist, so full of confidence, so full of promises to follow God throughout life, now becomes humble. He goes from a strong, bold confession to one of weakness, humility, petition, and prayer.

He acknowledges that he occasionally will deserve to be forsaken by God, but begs God not ever to forsake him "utterly." To be utterly forsaken by God is perhaps the ultimate definition of hell. The psalmist expresses confidence here that God will not ever utterly forsake him. We Christians know that this confidence has been justified by the work of Christ.

With the desperate plea comes the promise to obey God. You cannot go to God as a lazy beggar. He expects and deserves your obedience. However, obedience without prayer doesn't work any better than prayer without obedience.

Commit yourself to both obedience and prayer. When you go to God in humility, acknowledging His kingship and praising His righteousness, that is when He blesses you with mercy, peace, and salvation.

Lord, I know that You will never forsake me.
Help me daily to obey You!

CHAPTER TWO
Beth (verses 9-16)

PSALM 119

BETH
the House

MEDITATIONS

Beth, the House
(pronounced "beyt" or "bah-yeet")

Beth is the Hebrew word for house, tent, or family. It is one of the most important words in the Hebrew language, because it can refer to home, household, family, tribe, nation, or temple.

It has an important meaning to Christianity, as well. Beth-el is the house of God, the location of holiness on earth, or the meeting place of God and His people. It also represents Jesus as God incarnate, living on earth with His people.

Bethlehem means "house of bread," and Jesus, who is our bread of life, was born in Bethlehem! Moses was the faithful servant in God's house, but Jesus is the heir and the builder of His House. Jesus is also God's tabernacle among men. *Emmanuel* means "God with us." Jesus Himself *is* the House of the Lord God.

Jesus never needed or wanted a material home on earth, because He knew of a far more glorious home, and He came to open the door to that home for all of us. The Hebrew letter *beth* points to the Messiah, Who invites us all into His House!

Psalm 119
Verses 9-16

[9] *How can a young man keep his way pure?*
By living according to your word.
[10] *I seek you with all my heart;*
do not let me stray from your commands.
[11] *I have hidden your word in my heart*
that I might not sin against you.
[12] *Praise be to you, O LORD;*
teach me your decrees.
[13] *With my lips I recount*
all the laws that come from your mouth.
[14] *I rejoice in following your statutes*
as one rejoices in great riches.
[15] *I meditate on your precepts*
and consider your ways.
[16] *I delight in your decrees;*
I will not neglect your word.

Where Do You Live?

The Psalmist's Heart: Delight in the Word

These verses ask whether we prefer to live in the house of God's Word or in the house of the world. The psalmist is a young man, asking a young man's questions. The Hebrew word for *young* used here means "shaken off." He has been shaken off from the tender care of his parents. He has an inclination to follow God, but he is asking, "how?" He concludes that his strength is in God's Word—His Word for the present and His Word for the future.

He takes up God's Word, and hides it in his heart because he knows that this is the source of light, wisdom, and blessing. He will not neglect the Word, because it is such a delight. The word for *delight* used here means "I will skip about and jump for joy."

In spite of life's pain and suffering, the psalmist declares that he will not ever neglect God's precepts. He will meditate on His statutes and find joy and peace in their truth.

Your Walk in the Word: The Path of Meditation

Meditation makes your mind wise, your affections warm, your soul fat and flourishing, and your conversation fruitful. Meditation also inspires obedience.

You must not be careless. The path on which the Lord leads you is narrow, and slippery from the washing of the water of the Word. The Word is the soap and water which will wash and scour you along the way. The results are well worth the walk!

Out of meditation comes delight. Soon, you will not have to force yourself into the Word—you will be drawn to its power to free you from the chains of the world.

Your Walk in the World: The Treasure on the Coffee Table

Where is your treasure? The world puts its treasure in the bank. The Christian keeps his treasure inside his heart. The treasures of the world are perishable. Food in the cupboard can mold, be eaten by bugs, and go to waste. Once taken into the body, it is free from danger. When you take soul food into your heart, it is free from all hazards.

Eve was not snared as long as she kept her faith in the Word of God. She resisted Satan until she doubted the Word; that's when she became snared. The world is full of such snares, and you must keep the Word stored in your heart to be safe from the snares of the world.

Jesus said that you will come to love those things you think about and spend time contemplating. Worldly treasures take time and energy to attain, yet they can be stolen or destroyed in an instant. Put the same time and energy into God's treasures, and you will have a treasure that lasts forever. The treasure of God's Word can never be stolen from you. It will never rot or decay.

When you get the Word inside you, it is more precious than any worldly treasure on your coffee table!

His Gift for You: Treasure in Your Heart

Isn't it wonderful that God has provided a priceless treasure for us that is neither created by prosperous circumstances, nor destroyed by difficult situations? The soul that goes after the Word of God finds the true delight in life.

Dear Lord,
Thank You for the priceless treasure of Your Word. Draw me toward Your precepts, so that I may joyfully read and store up Your Word in my heart every single day. Help me to hear You speaking to my heart as I seek You. Let me receive the peace and joy that You have prepared for me. Guide me in Your truth and teach me, for You are God my Savior, and my hope is in You all day long.

Amen

DEVOTIONS

Day 9

A Young Man's Heart

⁹ How can a young man keep his way pure?
By living according to your word.

There is a desire in the heart of each of us to do the right thing—we want to live a good and pure life. Often, though, our high aspirations get lost somewhere in the day-to-day distractions of the world. This is not strictly a modern problem. Thousands of years ago, the psalmist asked God for direction on how to keep his way pure, and in this verse he shares with us the answer God gave him.

Only one thing can safeguard the purity of our way: living according to God's Word. When we learn and follow God's precepts, we are afforded protection from the contamination of the world. If we "do our own thing," and make our own decisions without God's guidance, we forfeit that protection. It is God's will that we abandon our own desires and ambitions, ignore the motives of men, and dedicate ourselves to His intentions. The world has changed a lot since God spoke to the psalmist's heart, but God's Word has not changed. In an imperfect world—whether ancient or modern—His was, is, and will always be the only perfect way!

Lord, show me the impurities in my life, and help
me to live in Your Word.

Day 10

A Seeking Heart

¹⁰ I seek you with all my heart;
do not let me stray from your commands.

Do you read your Bible with your head or with your heart? Head knowledge provides information about what God wants, but heart knowledge inspires a desire to serve Him.

God alone sees your heart, and your heart alone can see God. When your heart cries out to God for His guidance and wisdom, God answers. Our own free will often urges us to stray. If you give your whole heart to God, holding nothing back of your own, then you will not *want* to stray.

Not only must we seek out the hidden treasure, but we must take the treasure and hide it in our hearts. When you read God's Word, according to Proverbs 2:10, *"…wisdom will enter your heart, and knowledge will be pleasant to your soul."*

If you seek God with your whole heart, with everything you have and are, then He will be there to strengthen and guide you. He will help you to obey His commands; He will lead you on the righteous path.

Lord, give me a heart that seeks only You.

Day 11

Hide the Word in Your Heart

*¹¹ I have hidden your word in my heart
that I might not sin against you.*

The Word is your greatest protection from the world. If it is hidden deep in your heart, no one can take it away from you.

How do you hide the Word in your heart? You meditate on the Word: repeat a verse over and over in your mind. You pray: talk to Him intimately and hear the Word that He speaks to you. You pray the Word: say the things to God that He wants to hear from you.

Memorizing puts the Word in your head, but praying and meditating puts the Word in your heart. When the Word is in your heart, you are transformed into the person God meant you to be.

When the Word is hidden in your heart, your very being belongs to Him. The desire of the flesh to sin against God will be gone, and you will find joy in following Him. The Word in your heart will bring peace into your life.

Lord, fill my entire being, everything that I am, with Your Word.

Day 12

A Submissive Heart

¹² Praise be to you, O LORD; teach me your decrees.

The psalmist starts this verse with praise. Praise opens you up to the heart and mind of God, and prepares your heart to learn. We are commanded to praise God from morning to night: it is the path to God. Psalms 22:26 says *"...they who seek the LORD will praise him...."*

Decrees begin as the decisions of someone in authority. When you praise God, you become hungry to know and to follow the decisions that God has made. You become submissive to His will, and your spirit opens to Him so that He can teach you.

When we are proud of our own accomplishments, then our hearts are closed to God. When we praise Him, we submit ourselves to Him. Only when we pray, "Thy will be done," can He lead us in His perfect way.

The decrees of the Lord cannot be learned by reading and studying. You cannot speak to God's heart with your intellect. Instead, praise Him with your whole heart. Submit your will to His. Only an open and submissive heart can understand His Spirit.

Lord, I praise Your name with all my heart, and submit my will to Yours.

Day 13

An Abundant Heart

¹³ With my lips I recount all the laws that come from your mouth.

When the heart is full of the Word, the lips just have to speak out of an abundance of joy. The Lord is the fountain of all blessing.

The word *law* here means "teaching." The teachings of God are the Old and New Testaments. When you are immersed in the Word, then your mouth will be filled with the teachings of the Lord, and whenever you speak, your words will reflect the wisdom and love of God.

The psalmist knew that it was God's intention that the Word inhabit you and you live in the Word. Deuteronomy 30:14 teaches *"No, the word is very near you; it is in your mouth and in your heart so you may obey it."* Keep the Word near you at all times, in your heart and in your mouth. Repeat it, pray it, meditate upon it, and make it part of you.

Then, guard your speech to be sure that it reflects the Word in you. *Thank You, Lord, for Your Word. Let the words of my lips reflect You.*

Day 14

A Rejoicing Heart

14 I rejoice in following your statutes as one rejoices in great riches.

Have you ever dreamed of winning the lottery? Can you imagine the happiness of knowing that all your worldly needs are met? The psalmist knew that riches like that are fleeting. They can be stolen. They can decay.

He prayed for the riches of God's statutes, because he knew that God's Word takes care of all the needs of the soul. Worldly riches may bring personal enjoyment, but God's riches produce the highest kind of joy. You may think that worldly wealth would improve you, but God's statutes are the ultimate teachers.

The singer here rejoices not just in the statutes themselves, but in following them—in living them out in his own life. When you read God's Word, do you then strive to live those Words each day? The singer of this verse recognized that such a life was the greatest wealth you can possibly achieve.

Lord, I praise Your Name, for You have provided great riches for me.

Day 15

A Respectful Heart

15 I meditate on your precepts and consider your ways.

Christians lead two lives. One is the contemplative life, which consists of the time we spend praying, reading the Word, meditating. The other is the active life, the one which we live in this world.

The psalmist knew the importance of the contemplative life in preparing us to face the world. He meditated on God's precepts constantly—he was immersed in God.

Precepts here means "instructions"—instructions from the boss! We will follow God's instructions if we truly view Him as the boss—if we truly respect Him as the king, the head, the leader. Search your heart to discover the level of respect you hold for God.

Then, when you meditate upon His Word, remember that these are instructions from your perfect Creator.

Lord, I respect You as the teacher of
perfect instruction for my heart and my life.

Day 16

An Obedient Heart

16 I delight in your decrees; I will not neglect your word.

When you do what you know God wants you to, do you take delight in the doing? Do you get a good feeling when you take time from your hectic work schedule to help a coworker iron out a problem? Do you enjoy the energetic bustle of getting yourself or your family ready for church on Sunday morning? Being obedient to the urgings of God brings real joy—the same warm, happy satisfaction you may have felt as a child when you surprised your parents by performing an extra chore.

There are a lot of "I wills" in this psalm. The psalmist is a young man looking forward to a life of loving God. He recognizes that finding treasure can be a long, involved process—it takes time to dig a gold mine. He is willing to spend a lifetime waiting on the Lord, because he knows it will bring revelation, clarity—and joy.

Hand in hand with joyful obedience is attention to the Word. You cannot know what God wants for you if you are not in the Word, and you cannot know the great joy that He has promised without obedience to that Word.

Lord, help me to know the joy of true obedience to You.

CHAPTER THREE
Gimel (verses 17-24)

Gimel, the Burden Bearer
(pronounced "gim-mel")

Hebrew scholars define *gimel* as "to nourish until ripe." The shape of the letter is like the neck of a camel, an animal which serves man as a burden bearer. Just as the camel carries physical burdens, Jesus bore man's spiritual burdens—our sins, illnesses, sorrows, and grief (Isaiah 53:4,11).

The camel is not a lovely beast, but it is a useful one as men rely on it for survival in desert places. Jesus was the *"...root out of dry ground...*[Who had] *no beauty or majesty to attract us to him..."* (Isaiah 53:2).

Gimel also represents a weaned child who can go a long time without drinking. The prophet, Isaiah, foretold of Jesus' role as the source of living water (Isaiah 12:3; 44:3). Jesus confirmed this calling in John 4:13,14, when He said He would give us water that would well up to eternal life. In Jesus is stored all that we need as we travel through this dry, desolate world. Surely, Jesus is the greatest burden bearer man has ever known—the suffering servant, source of hidden reservoirs of life!

Psalm 119
Verses 17-24

¹⁷ *Do good to your servant, and I will live;*
I will obey your word.
¹⁸ *Open my eyes that I may see*
wonderful things in your law.
¹⁹ *I am a stranger on earth;*
do not hide your commands from me.
²⁰ *My soul is consumed with longing*
for your laws at all times.
²¹ *You rebuke the arrogant, who are cursed*
and who stray from your commands.
²² *Remove from me scorn and contempt,*
for I keep your statutes.
²³ *Though rulers sit together and slander me,*
your servant will meditate on your decrees.
²⁴ *Your statutes are my delight;*
they are my counselors.

Travels With the Master

The Psalmist's Heart: Yearning for God's Laws

In the eight "beth" verses, the psalmist prays as a youth, coming into the world with a heart longing for God. In these "gimel" verses, he prays as a pilgrim who finds himself a stranger in an enemy's country. The appeal here is to God alone, and the prayer is very direct and personal. His cry is for a bountiful provision from a loving Master. Without his Master's liberal grace and abundant mercy, he cannot live.

This is the song of a lonely person who feels abandoned by the world. He calls out to God. Eternal longing is reflected here: his soul is consumed with longing for God's Word. In the darkest hours, the faith that God is always there sustains this psalmist.

First, the psalmist promises to hide God's Word in his heart, and now he says, "Don't hide the Word from me, but open it up to me. Give me seeing eyes and hearing ears."

Jesus certainly had the Word hidden in Him. He constantly quoted the Word, and He told His disciples, *"...I have food to eat that you know nothing about"* (John 4:32). What was that food? It was the Word!

Your Walk in the Word: What is Your Desire?

There is great power in desire. What do you desire? Do you want to live God's Word or do your own thing? What do you wish for? What do you desire? Desires which can be put off and on like garments are at best mere wishes. Earthly desires are temporary emotions, born of excitement and doomed to die.

There is another longing which should be constant and eternal—the longing for God's revelation in every situation of your life. He is needed in your family, in your finances, in your physical body, and in your relationships.

Work for God, and you will be victorious over the enemy because He is working in you. Be consumed with a need for His Word.

The Bible is a wonderland of treasure and miracles. Which treasure do you desire—the world's treasure or God's treasure? Jesus told us that *"where your treasure is, there your heart will be also"* (Matthew 6:21). Seek the eternal treasure of God's Word with all your heart.

Your Walk in the World: Down on Your Knees

Pride does terrible things to men. Humility makes men like angels, but pride makes angels into devils. Look at the examples of prideful men in the Bible: Cain, Pharaoh, Nebuchadnezzar, Herod. Proud men like these never have any true friends. When they are prosperous, they don't know anybody. When adversity strikes, nobody knows them.

It takes great grace to keep us alive. Be cast down on your knees, so that you are not cast down upon your face!

His Gift for You: Miracles

The Lord treats His servants well. The scriptures teem with miracles. We are born blind, but we only have to ask, and God will remove the veil from our eyes and reveal His gifts.

Father,
Give me a heart that desires only Your treasures. Take the veil from my eyes, and let me see only You. Give me the strength and will to pursue Your Word each day, so that I may hide it in my heart as a protection from the enemy.

Amen

DEVOTIONS

GIMEL
the
Burden Bearer
MEDITATIONS

Day 17

Travel in Service

17 Do good to your servant, and I will live; I will obey your word.

A good master loves, protects, and rewards his servants. A good and faithful servant recognizes the fact that he has a good master, and is pleased to obey him, knowing he will be well cared for, and will thrive under that loving care. He knows his needs will be met and his efforts rewarded. He adores his master, feels privileged to serve him, and wants to be like him. He respects his master's decisions and follows them unquestioningly. What is more, he enjoys telling others how wonderful his master is, and is proud and happy to bring others into his master's service.

God is more than a good master—He is *the* good master. He does good to His servants, who live because of His goodness. It is a pleasure to obey Him, because we know He will only command us to do what is for our own good, and because we know He will reward us with His love and care. Trust your master; be obedient to Him; know that you are privileged to serve Him. There is no other honor higher than to be a member of His household.

Master, I want to serve You in everything I do.

Day 18

Travel With Unveiled Eyes

18 Open my eyes that I may see wonderful things in your law.

Perhaps the word "law" conjures a picture of dusty books, long-winded speeches, and rules that may seem boring or useless. If so, perhaps you—like the psalmist—should ask God to open your eyes to the marvelous beauty of His Word—the Law that governs all creation!

God's Law—His Word—is the center of the universe, and the foundation upon which all life is centered. As such, it is perfect, unchanging, unblemished, and beautiful. The Law is wonderful and desirable. It is the standard by which perfection is measured.

Ask God for spiritual perception. Ask Him to open your eyes so you can see the great beauty of His Word! Once you have seen and marveled at its beauty and completeness, you'll be unable to imagine your life without it!

Father, open my eyes to the wonder of Your Law.

Day 19

Travel in Truth and Wisdom

¹⁹ I am a stranger on earth; do not hide your commands from me.

We are all strangers in a strange land. Do you feel lost, as if you had been banished from your real home? You may feel like a stranger to others, but you are not a stranger to God. The psalmist finds reminders of home and a map showing the way home, when he studies God's Word. He doesn't want such precious words to be hidden from him.

Psalm 51:6 says that God wants His truth to live inside you. *"Surely you desire truth in the inner parts; you teach me wisdom in the inmost place."* When you hide the Word inside you, God can turn that into wisdom.

In order to receive that wisdom, you must be a stranger to the world. Your joys and rewards are in the salvation purchased by Jesus, not in the temporary things of this world. Only when you are separated from the ways of the world can you clearly see the path home.

Father, show me the ways of the world that are too much with me.

Day 20

Travel With Longing

²⁰ My soul is consumed with longing for your laws at all times.

One of the best ways to find out what people are really like is to examine their deepest longings. What do you want more than anything? A new car? A better job? The psalmist wanted to feed upon God's Word.

Once you have entered the world of God's Law, you become filled with a longing to know more and more. It is a bittersweet longing, because you become more aware of your own imperfections. God's forgiveness will become even more precious to you. What a wonderful journey it is!

Spend more time in the Word, and the secrets of His covenant will be revealed, opening like the petals of a miraculous flower. Let your soul be consumed with a longing for His truth.

Lord, I know that only You can fulfill the deepest longings of my heart.

Day 21

Travel Without Burdens

²¹ You rebuke the arrogant, who are cursed
and who stray from your commands.

This verse deals with a favorite tool of the enemy: pride. Pride is the "hidden" sin—but it's hidden only to you! God recognizes it immediately, and hates it the most. His Word teaches that proud men are cursed, and will be abased. He rebuked the pride of Pharaoh, first with plagues, and later, by closing the Red Sea to the Egyptians. Nobody blesses proud men; they soon become a burden even to themselves. Pride is a sin which ultimately causes torment.

When arrogant people make you unhappy, take comfort in the fact that God has the same quarrel. He knows that arrogant men eventually become disobedient. They begin to trust their own judgment instead of God's commands.

Search your heart for strongholds of pride. Can you really "let go and let God" or do you continually try to manage things on your own? Pride will cause you to stray from God's commands. Guard against it by taking on the shield of faith. *"...take up the shield of faith, with which you can extinguish all the flaming arrows of the evil one"* (Ephesians 6:16).

Lord, protect me against arrogance. Help me to trust and obey You.

Day 22

Travel With Blessings

²² Remove from me scorn and contempt, for I keep your statutes.

Scorn and contempt had been heaped upon the psalmist. Has this ever happened to you? It is a painful experience to be slandered and despised. It is an affliction of a world ruled by the enemy. If you ask Him, God will either remove the affliction, or he will take away the sting.

If you try to clear things up yourself (another act of pride!), you will usually fail. When you are attacked, take it before the highest court. Leave it to the judge of the whole earth. He can rebuke the proud accuser. Be quiet and let Him plead your case.

What can you do? You should turn to the Word. You can keep God's testimonies all the time you are being scorned. Remember what Jesus told you: *"But I tell you: Love your enemies and pray for those who persecute you"* (Matthew 5:44). When you pray for your enemies, you will begin to see them as God sees them. What enemies have you prayed for today?

Father, bless my enemies' lives as You have blessed mine,
and help me to love them as You do.

Day 23

Travel in Peace

23 Though rulers sit together and slander me,
your servant will meditate on your decrees.

A good conscience is the best security for a good man. His enemies may talk against him, but what does he do while they're slandering him? He meditates on God's Word. God's Word is the greatest key to personal peace; the barbs and arrows of men's words cannot pierce the protection it provides you.

Are you meditating on God's Word, or on the words that people say against you? Don't meditate on the devil, or on your circumstances, or on your wounds and hurts. That kind of meditation will defeat you. Meditate on the right thing: God's Word.

While rulers are sitting to reproach the psalmist, the psalmist is sitting with God. You should do the same when faced with adversity. If you feed on the Word, you grow strong and peaceful, and you'll be protected from the sting of tongues.

Remember that Jesus Himself was slandered throughout His ministry, but even when He was brought before Pilate, He did not react with anger or scorn. He did not try to defend Himself. He knew that God would justify Him and defeat those false accusations.

Lord, take away my bitterness toward those
who are lying about me, and give me Your peace.

Day 24

Travel to Your Desires

²⁴ Your statutes are my delight; they are my counselors.

You may face seasons of affliction, but you do not have to be defeated by them. The psalmist found his delight and guidance in the testimony of God.

Have you ever been the victim of gossip, or felt the stinging of words spoken behind your back? Perhaps you have even been slandered so badly that friends urged you to stand up for yourself and go to court. You may not need a costly lawyer to buy back your peace of mind if, like the psalmist, you let God's statutes be your counselors.

In life's greatest sorrows, let His statutes be your delight and your guide. Let them advise you. Give more time to the true testimonies of the Lord than to the false witness of your foes. The Lord promises that if you will delight yourself in Him, He will give you the desires of your heart.

Lord, Your Word is my defender, my counselor, and my advisor. Your Word will vindicate me against those who mean me harm.

CHAPTER FOUR
Daleth (verses 25-32)

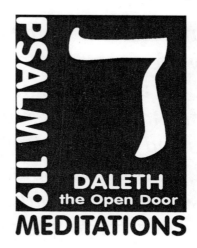

PSALM 119

DALETH
the Open Door

MEDITATIONS

Daleth, the Open Door
(pronounced "day-lett")

Most Hebrew scholars define *daleth* as an open door which serves as either an entrance or an exit. Often, *daleth* is a swinging door, like a gate.

In ancient times, the gates of a city opened in the morning so that people could go out to their fields to work and accomplish their business. At night, the people came back in, and the gates of the city were closed to protect them. We are told that in the New Jerusalem, the gates will never be closed, day or night, because there will be nothing to fear—nothing that can harm us.

Daleth might also represent the door to the pen where shepherds kept their lambs. The sheep could go out of that swinging door to the pastures, and then return to the pen for safety at night. Jesus told us that He would be that door for us: *"...I tell you the truth, I am the gate for the sheep...I am the gate; whoever enters through me will be saved. He will come in and go out, and find pasture"* (John 10:7,9).

Psalm 119
Verses 25-32

²⁵ I am laid low in the dust;
preserve my life according to your word.
²⁶ I recounted my ways and you answered me;
teach me your decrees.
²⁷Let me understand the teaching of your precepts;
then I will meditate on your wonders.
²⁸ My soul is weary with sorrow;
strengthen me according to your word.
²⁹ Keep me from deceitful ways;
be gracious to me through your law.
³⁰ I have chosen the way of truth;
I have set my heart on your laws.
³¹ I hold fast to your statutes, O LORD;
do not let me be put to shame.
³² I run in the path of your commands,
for you have set my heart free.

Coming Out of Grief and Pain

The Psalmist's Heart: Seeking Joy From the Depths

In these eight verses, the psalmist expresses deep depression. He is brought low; his face is in the dust; his soul is weary. Does he give up? No! He knows that the door out of his grief and depression is the Word of God.

Even when he feels helpless and hopeless, the psalmist remembers the promises of the Word. He holds fast to the belief that if he stays in the Word, his reward will be joy and thanksgiving.

What a deep and wonderful faith he exhibits as he seeks God's precepts from the depths of sorrow and gloom!

Your Walk in the Word: Behind Closed Doors

When Elisha raised a boy from the dead, he went into his room and closed the door behind him (II Kings 4:33). Some of the most important events in Jesus' ministry occurred behind closed doors: the healing of Jairus' daughter (Mark 5:40), the Last Supper, and Christ's first and second appearances to the disciples after the resurrection (John 20:19,26).

Jesus often sought to get away from the world and its crowds. He began His ministry with 40 days of solitude, and spent His last hours of freedom on this earth alone in prayer.

Jesus told us to imitate Him. *"But when you pray, go into your room, close the door and pray to your Father, who is unseen. Then your Father, who sees what is done in secret, will reward you"* (Matthew 6:6). Behind closed doors, when you seek God in solitude, He will be there to answer and comfort you.

Your Walk in the World: Keep the Door of My Lips

The psalmist seems concerned about the doors in his life. He repeatedly asks God to guard these doors. He wants God's help to keep evil from entering his life.

The mouth is a "door" about which we need to be concerned. Out of that door can come cruelty, impurity, jealousy...a whole host of the enemy's tools. We should all cry, *"Set a guard over my mouth, O LORD; keep watch over the door of my lips"* (Psalm 141:3).

A door can keep evil out while allowing good things to pass through. Evil is lurking at every door, and we must always be on guard: *"...sin is crouching at your door; it desires to have you, but you must master it"* (Genesis 4:7).

Are the words that come out of your mouth good or damaging? Do you criticize too much? Do you complain? Do you gossip? Ask God to guard the door of your mouth, and allow nothing to pass through unless it glorifies Him.

His Gift for You: Life

The Word brings life in the face of death and light in the face of darkness. In your worst trials, you have only to choose and cleave to God's Word.

Father,
Thank You for being here with me always, even when I am laid low in the dust and my soul is weary with sorrow. Place in my heart a yearning for You that is stronger than any worldly grief or pain. Give me a heart that longs for You, that hungers for Your Word, and seeks to learn and understand Your precepts. I lift Your Name in thanksgiving, for You have set my heart free.

Amen

DEVOTIONS

PSALM 119

DALETH
the Open Door

MEDITATIONS

Day 25

Out of the Dust

²⁵ *I am laid low in the dust; preserve my life according to your word.*

This verse is pregnant with pain. The psalmist is overwhelmed, but does he look for pity? No, he goes after the Word. He believes the Word will bring life.

Have you ever felt so low that you were ready to die? Have you been choked by the dust of this world? We humans seem to cling to the earth. There is a tendency of the soul to cleave to earthly things. We are all pulled toward the dust.

God made man from dust, and then He breathed life into him. It is that life which you must seek every day. Seek the life-giving Word, and you will shake off the dust of the world. You will be made into God's new creation.

Dear God, send me running each day to Your life-giving Word.

Day 26

Out of Your Hands

²⁶ *I recounted my ways and you answered me; teach me your decrees.*

To *recount* means to "tell or describe in detail." It must have been an emotional experience for the psalmist to approach God and describe his own ways in detail. It must have been even more emotional to hear and understand God's answer—His judgment. Though the psalmist does not report exactly what God showed him, the message comes through loud and clear: man's way is not God's way. The psalmist, without bitterness, pride, or anger, admits immediately that his only hope lies in learning God's decrees.

Take some time to recount your ways to God, and listen to His answer. It will help you line up your life with God's will. Of course, God knows your innermost secrets anyway—this confession is less to inform Him about yourself, than to help you recognize your own shortcomings, and to open your heart to receive His guidance. The more you seek God's will, the more He will teach you—and the stronger your hunger will grow to seek Him more!

Dear Lord, I want to put my life in Your hands,
and align it with Your will.

Day 27

Out of Ignorance

27 *Let me understand the teaching of your precepts;*
    then I will meditate on your wonders.

This verse is often called "The Student's Prayer." God would like us all to be students of the most important subject of all: His precepts. You can have no higher goal than to understand God's Word. It is a lifelong journey. It is a journey of untold rewards.

The psalmist understands that the Word pours fresh life into us. The revealed Word brings the revealed will of God. The Word is your comfort because its words bring you light, liberty, and food for your soul, as well as weapons for your spiritual warfare. Lovers of Scripture have everything they need.

When we read about God, we become more like Him. The Bible leads us in this direction. The godly are like candles: they can light each other.

Father, I want to be a student of Your ways all my life.

Day 28

Out of Depression

28 *My soul is weary with sorrow;*
    strengthen me according to your word.

Depression is not a sudden thing. It is a gradual process, a drawing down to the earth. It is so exhausting that it wearies even the soul.

The heaviness of depression can turn life into a long death. Our tears are a distillation of the heart. When you weep, your soul wastes away. Have you come under heaviness like this? Often, it comes again and again. You may feel as if you have been poured out like water and spilled upon the ground.

When you are in such a state of pain and exhaustion, where can you turn? The only sure source of strength is the Word. Depression comes from the world, but relief comes from the Word. Immerse yourself in the loving promises of the living Lord. It is so wonderful to be strengthened by the Word!

Lord, I know that only You can fulfill the deepest longings of my heart.

Day 29

Out of Deceit

[29]   *Keep me from deceitful ways; be gracious to me through your law.*

Deceit means promising one thing, and then delivering another. Many worldly pleasures are deceitful in nature; often wealth and fame promise happiness—but deliver depression, despair—even death.

The opposite of deceit is truth. Jesus is the Truth, and only His ways are trustworthy. The psalmist asks God to keep him from deceitful ways, because he realizes that he has a tendency to be a little dishonest with others, with himself—maybe even with God. We all have that tendency inside us.

If you excuse your tendency to live according to the world instead of according to the Word, that is like trying to con God. God is not fooled when he hears someone explain, "I'm a good person—I have a good heart, so it doesn't matter if I don't read the Bible, or go to church, or spend time in prayer each day." God cannot be conned—so it's best to be honest from the outset. Remember, He has already forgiven you—you only need to talk to Him honestly.

Lord, protect me from the deceitful ways of the world.
I want to follow Your truth.

Day 30

Out of Deception

30 I have chosen the way of truth; I have set my heart on your laws.

Have you chosen the way of truth? It is not always easy. We have a lying nature inside us, and it is easy to slip into little deceptions. Those little deceptions pile upon each other, until we begin to believe our own lies! If you are feeling overwhelmed, consider carefully whether you have allowed your lying nature to overcome your spiritual desire for truth.

God's Word is the way to complete truth but, like the psalmist, you must *choose* to follow it. God has given us His laws, but He doesn't force us to follow them; He lets us choose. Fill your heart with His Word—set your heart on His laws—and there will be no room left for the little dishonesties that can blind you to the path. You'll automatically be headed in the right direction!

Father, thank You for sending Your Son
to show us the path to the truth.

Day 31

Out of Shame

31 I hold fast to your statutes, O LORD; do not let me be put to shame.

There are three kinds of truth: truth in heart, in word, and in deed. Have you put the truth of the Word into your heart? Have you dedicated yourself to pursuing that truth? If you have, then your deeds will reflect the truth.

The psalmist has made the connection here. He knows that if he holds onto God's truth, then his deeds will not shame him. Does that mean that the world will applaud what he does? Of course not—the world lives in deceit.

Deeds done on the foundation of the truth of God's statutes will please the Lord. Deeds done on the foundation of the world's lies will bring His censure.

You do not have the power to do righteous deeds without the help of God. Hold fast to His truth, and you will not be put to shame before Him.

In the name of Jesus, whose name is Truth,
let me not be put to shame.

Day 32

Out of Disobedience

32 I run in the path of your commands,
for you have set my heart free.

In this verse, the psalmist celebrates with a new resolve. His soul may be weary, and he may be laid low, but he knows that God is the answer. Notice how he approaches God. He doesn't creep or crawl—*he runs!*

Are you running to God? Do you sometimes loiter? Are you standing still on the path? Perhaps you are too distracted by worldly things. Take a lesson from this psalmist who *runs* in the path of truth. Dedicate your time and attention to the path of God's commands.

Athletes must have strong, healthy hearts, and running strengthens them. In the same way, when you meditate upon God's Word, your heart becomes full of joy and understanding. Then, as you run in the path of truth, God will strengthen that joy and understanding more and more.

Lord, set my heart free, so that I may run
in the path of obedience to You.

CHAPTER FIVE
He (verses 33-40)

He, the Window
(pronounced "hay")

This letter can mean "ventilation," "lattice," or "breathing room." It represents the times in which God gives us a little breathing room. It is a reminder that there is a window to God—that window is Jesus Christ.

The first window mentioned in the Bible is the window which Noah built into the ark. God told him to put a window in the top of the ark. From that window, Noah could not look down or sideways, he could only look up toward God.

Today, we have that same window in Jesus. Through Him, we see the light of His kingdom. Jesus brings a beautiful light into our lives.

Psalm 119
Verses 33-40

[33] Teach me, O LORD, to follow your decrees;
then I will keep them to the end.
[34] Give me understanding,
and I will keep your law
and obey it with all my heart.
[35] Direct me in the path of your commands,
for there I find delight.
[36] Turn my heart toward your statutes
and not toward selfish gain.
[37] Turn my eyes away from worthless things;
preserve my life according to your word.
[38] Fulfill your promise to your servant,
so that you may be feared.
[39] Take away the disgrace I dread,
for your laws are good.
[40] How I long for your precepts!
Preserve my life in your righteousness.

Get a Grip

The Psalmist's Heart: A Plea for Guidance

The psalmist cries out for God's will to be revealed. At the same time, he worries that he might be unable to understand God's directives. He's concerned that he might be blinded by the things of the world.

He knows that only God can give him clear guidance and teaching. No one can teach a man who refuses to learn, so he needs not only the teaching, but the will to learn. He requires understanding.

The Law of Jehovah is to be set before the hand, the eyes, the mind, the feet, and the heart:

- *Teach me* in verse 33 literally means "to send out the hand." Imagine that God is pointing to show you the way.
- *Give me understanding* in verse 34 is asking for the Word to be set before the mind.
- In verse 35, the *feet* are to follow the narrow path that God has pointed out.
- In verse 36, the *heart* is to be turned toward the Word and away from the world.
- In verse 37, the *eyes* are to turn to the life-giving Word.

Your Walk in the Word: Take Hold of the Things of God

It is with the heart that we must take hold of the things of God. Like the psalmist, resolve to observe God's revelations with your whole heart.

Your life will lean the way your heart leans. The way to cure a leaning in the wrong direction is to bend the soul the opposite way. God can bend you back in the right direction, if you ask Him to do it.

Those who are taught of God will never forget their lessons. Depend on the continual teaching of the Lord. As God keeps teaching you, you will become better equipped to keep His way. If you receive the living, incorruptible seed of the Word, you will live. With a heart that receives the teaching of the Lord, you have full, abundant life!

Your Walk in the World: Blinded by Covetousness

In these verses, the singer asks God to turn him away from covetousness. Covetousness is a common sin, but very few people really confess it. When your heart is full of something other than God, you often cannot see your own faults or your own greed.

Sin first entered man's mind through the eye, and it is still the favorite gate for Satan. Turn your eyes away from sin, and behold the face of God. There, the real treasure will be found.

The Law of Jehovah may be right before your eyes, but you won't see it if your eyes are focused on worthless things.

His Gift for You: A Renewed Heart

These verses are the petitions of a renewed heart. God has given you a breathing space...a time to learn...a time to turn your heart and mind and eyes toward God.

Lord,
Thank You for Your knowledge, the knowledge of life. Show me the way that You would have me follow. Turn my eyes from the temptations of the world. Guard my heart from love of the world, for I want to give my whole heart to You. I know that people are destroyed for lack of knowledge of Your Word, and I praise the living God who has created me, taught me, and is leading me on the right path. Yours is the gracious way, the way of light and life. I want to dedicate my life to living in Your glorious light.

Amen

DEVOTIONS

PSALM 119

HE
the Window

MEDITATIONS

Day 33

Get God's Instruction

33 Teach me, O LORD, to follow your decrees;
then I will keep them to the end.

Have you ever made a "New Year's resolution" or a promise to change something you dislike about yourself? Even with the best intentions, this can be difficult. You mentally outline a plan of action, and may even succeed for a while before slipping back into old habits.

The psalmist recognizes that he is helpless to better himself without God's assistance. He petitions God for the gift of obedience, realizing his need to do things God's way. Once he learns to follow God's decrees, he has no doubt he will be able to prevail "to the very end." He does not put his faith in his own will power or good intentions, but tells God, "I need *You* to teach me how to do this."

There can be no righteousness without teaching from God. You cannot do it alone, and God doesn't expect you to do it alone. Call on Him for the training, teaching, and guidance that you need to excel.

Dear God, give me a teachable heart, and guide me on Your path.

Day 34

Get God's Understanding

34 Give me understanding, and I will keep your law
and obey it with all my heart.

One of the most important lessons God teaches us is to trust in Him. When the psalmist asks for "understanding" here, he is not asking for his own understanding, but for God's. Proverbs 3:5 cautions us: *"Trust in the LORD with all your heart and lean not on your own understanding...."*

How often have you taken on the burdens of life all by yourself? Your life becomes much easier when you trust God's understanding. He knows exactly what you need. He has a perfect plan for your life. He is just waiting for you to stop attempting to control things yourself.

Isn't it time to appoint Him the leader of your life? When you understand that He is in charge, you will follow Him joyfully. Your heart will desire nothing less.

*Dear Lord, fill my heart with a longing
for Your understanding, and not my own.*

Day 35

Get On the Right Path

35 Direct me in the path of your commands, for there I find delight.

This verse is another plea for leadership and direction from God. The psalmist asks God to direct him on the right path. Notice that the way of God is not a four-lane highway, but a path. Though it is taken by few people, the psalmist longs for that path, and finds his greatest delight in following it.

The psalmist visualized the path described in Proverbs 4:18: *"The path of the righteous is like the first gleam of dawn, shining ever brighter till the full light of day."* We cannot find that delightful path by ourselves. We must ask God to show us the way. Psalm 119 refers to this path six times.

Jesus is our leader on this path of light. He came *"to shine on those living in darkness and in the shadow of death, to guide our feet into the path of peace"* (Luke 1:79). We only need to follow Him. As the path twists and turns through life, it branches off in many directions. We may lose sight of Jesus ahead of us, and lose our way. We need to pause at every turn and, like the psalmist, ask God for further direction.

Father, direct me along the path of Your precious Son.

Day 36

Get Turned Toward God

36 Turn my heart toward your statutes and not toward selfish gain.

Coupled with the next verse, this verse depicts a combination found frequently in the Old Testament: the heart and the eyes. Man is directed by the inner self (the leanings of the heart) as well as by the external world (the attractions of the eye).

Like the eyes, the heart has the ability to focus. It may focus in on God, or on selfish desires. Even the Word of God can be used selfishly, to justify wrong actions. Some Christians may profess to believe, hoping to gain the blessings of God, yet never really focus on God's Word with their hearts. Focusing your eyes on the Word externally will bear no fruit, unless you focus your heart on the Word at the same time.

If you truly desire to know and worship God, focus your heart on God's Word, rather than on your own needs. God is waiting for you to turn to Him with love and praise. Ask Him to work in you to keep your heart leaning in the right direction.

Lord, I desire only to know You and to love You.

Day 37

Get Focused

37 Turn my eyes away from worthless things;
preserve my life according to your word.

This verse mentions the second half of the Old Testament duo: heart and eyes. The eyes can become a tool of the enemy if he can get you to focus them on worthless things. Worthless things are dead things; they cannot give you life. Eyes focused on the world admit darkness and death. Eyes focused on the Word admit light and life.

When we allow our eyes to be focused on greed, selfishness, lust, or any of the traps of this world, it is easy for the enemy to lead us on the road to death. Where are your eyes focused?

The eyes are the window through which the external world enters. Are you admitting lifeless things or are you admitting the light of the truth, the Word of God? The psalmist does not claim to have the ability to focus on God by himself. He asks for God's help. Ask God to guard your eyes from the distractions of the world.

Lord, turn my eyes away from the world.
I want to live in Your Word!

Day 38

Get Promises Fulfilled

38 Fulfill your promise to your servant, so that you may be feared.

When the Word is promised in part, then performance of the whole is assured. Paul talks about one promise that was fulfilled to him. *"But the Lord stood at my side and gave me strength, so that through me the message might be fully proclaimed and all the Gentiles might hear it. And I was delivered from the lion's mouth"* (II Timothy 4:17).

As a result of that promise fulfilled, Paul could express confident hope in the rest of the promise. *"The Lord will rescue me from every evil attack and will bring me safely to his heavenly kingdom. To him be glory for ever and ever. Amen"* (II Timothy 4:18).

There are a lot of promises that God fulfills daily in our lives. Your experience today is going to give you confidence in what is to come.

Father, I exalt You, for Your Word and
Your promises have proven Your almightiness!

Day 39

Get Going

39 Take away the disgrace I dread, for your laws are good.

There are two kinds of judgment: man's and God's. The psalmist recognizes that God's Law is superior and inherently good. He knows that if he lives by the Word of God, he never needs to fear disgrace by earthly standards. If he walks in the ways of God, other men will respect him.

Even more importantly, the psalmist dreads falling into disgrace with God—not because he fears God, but because he knows God's laws are good and, for that fact alone, are worthy of being obeyed. In earlier verses, the psalmist asked for God's laws to be revealed to him. Then he asked for an understanding of God's laws, and asked God to make him obedient to them. This verse marks a turning point for the psalmist: he has come to love the Law.

As we turn to God more and more for wisdom, understanding, and the gift of obedience, we will come to love His Word.

Thank You, Lord, for the perfection of Your laws. They lift me above disgrace and judgment. They are worthy of my obedience.

Day 40

Get Life From the Word

40 How I long for your precepts!
Preserve my life in your righteousness.

The righteousness of God refers to the faithfulness with which He acts. He keeps His commitments. It also refers to His kingship—the perfect power which protects the helpless. The believer longs for God's Word, because it is the revelation of the righteousness of God upon which all life depends.

As a Christian, your path to God's righteousness is Jesus. *"This righteousness from God comes through faith in Jesus Christ to all who believe…"* (Romans 3:22). Jesus has justified you before God's perfect judgment, assuring you of eternal life.

What heart does not melt at the thought of the price Jesus paid for our salvation? Our grateful love for Him leads us to a longing to know Him more intimately, and in that longing, we turn to His precepts: the Bible!

Turn your heart and your eyes to Him, and know the blessings of a righteous God.

Oh, righteous God, thank You for sending
Your Son to purchase my salvation.

CHAPTER SIX
Waw (verses 41-48)

PSALM 119
WAW
Nail
MEDITATIONS

Waw, Nail
(pronounced "vahv")

Waw is the Hebrew word for "and." It is used widely in Hebrew, often to begin sentences and paragraphs. Hebrew scholars liken *waw* to a nail which connects two ideas together.

Each one of these eight verses begin with *waw*. This couldn't have been easy to write, because *waw* is a conjunction in Hebrew, and there are almost no words that begin with that letter. It would be a little like trying to write an eight verse poem all beginning with the letter "Z" in English.

Psalm 119
Verses 41-48

⁴¹ *May your unfailing love come to me, O LORD,*
your salvation according to your promise;
⁴² *then I will answer the one who taunts me,*
for I trust in your word.
⁴³ *Do not snatch the word*
of truth from my mouth,
for I have put my hope in your laws.
⁴⁴ *I will always obey your law, for ever and ever.*
⁴⁵ *I will walk about in freedom,*
for I have sought out your precepts.
⁴⁶ *I will speak of your statutes before kings*
and will not be put to shame,
⁴⁷ *for I delight in your commands*
because I love them.
⁴⁸ *I lift up my hands to your commands,*
which I love,
and I meditate on your decrees.

Nailed to a Sure Place

The Psalmist's Heart: Godly Men Give Back

This octave consists of petitions and promises. Verses 41 and 43 are petitions, and the other six are promises.

There is a big difference between godly men and ungodly men. All men seek good things from God, but the wicked do not want to give Him anything in return. They are motivated out of love of themselves and not love of the Lord. They want to receive, but they don't care to give God glory.

The psalmist had two requests to make of God, but in return he made six promises to God. This is a three-to-one exchange! Godly men love God so much that they continually strive to give Him more and more.

Your Walk in the Word: Jesus is the Nail

One use of the letter *waw* is to refer to someone or something as being "nailed in a sure place." Eliakim, who was placed by God as the king's steward and served both Hezekiah and Isaiah, was "nailed in a sure place" when he became the steward (Isaiah 22:23).

The Romans surely thought they had nailed Jesus to a sure place when they put Him on the cross. No man could free himself from those nails and live to tell about it—yet that is exactly what Jesus did!

Jesus freed you, too, from the nails of sin and death. He became the holy nail that surely fastened you to salvation and eternal life. He is God's nail—and on Him we hang our hope.

Your Walk in the World: Speak Boldly

In these verses, the psalmist recognizes his responsibility as a witness. He wants to have an answer for the man who reproaches him. He desires to speak testimonies of the Lord before kings. He knows the only way he can do this is by having true familiarity with the Law of God.

He seeks freedom from fear, so he can speak about God before kings. It is not enough to hold the Word in your heart and to cherish the wonderful blessings that God bestows upon His believers. You must "nail" the message to others by telling them the wonderful story of salvation. When you tell others, you are nailing down your own salvation, too.

The psalmist asks God to give him courage, and with that courage, he promises to carry the wonderful message to others.

His Gift for You: Freedom

Nothing is more glorious than the freedom from sin which Jesus purchased for you. Through it, God bestows the courage to witness so others, too, may be saved. What a wondrous and wonderful plan!

Thank You, Jesus,
For the terrible price You paid when You were nailed to a tree just for me. It takes my breath away to know that You loved me enough to suffer that way! With Your suffering, You purchased my freedom —a most incredible gift. Now I ask You to give me the courage to speak up and tell others about You, so that your great gift can be shared with the world. Together, we can "nail" many new believers to the "sure place" of salvation.

Amen

DEVOTIONS

PSALM 119
WAW
Nail
MEDITATIONS

Day 41

Nailed to the Cross

*⁴¹ May your unfailing love come to me, O LORD,
your salvation according to your promise;*

Do you long for God's love? Do you imagine how wonderful it will be when Jesus returns? The psalmist was still looking for the first coming of the Messiah Who would bring salvation when He came. Today, you can bask in the salvation that has already been purchased, yet there is still a longing for the unfailing love of God.

Salvation is the greatest gift to come out of God's love for you. You need His love, you need His mercy, and most of all, you need His salvation.

How wonderful that God knew what you needed even before you were born! He provided for your greatest needs through His Son, Jesus!

Dear God, how I cherish Your unfailing love for me.

Day 42

Nail the Taunters

*⁴² then I will answer the one who taunts me,
for I trust in your word.*

There are three sorts of blasphemers: the devil, heretics, and slanderers.
- The devil is answered by an internal word of humility.
- Heretics are answered by an external word of wisdom.
- Slanderers are answered by an active word of a good life.

You know the devil would like to take the Word out of your mouth, just like he takes the seed of the Word from the path, lest it should bring forth fruit (Matthew 13:19). This is why we must hold fast the confession of our faith without wavering. We must be faithful to Him Who is so faithful to us.

Dear Lord, strengthen Your Word in me;
it is my defense against heretics, slanderers, and the devil.

Day 43

Nail the Right Words

43 Do not snatch the word of truth from my mouth,
for I have put my hope in your laws.

Have you ever opened your mouth to tell someone about Christ, and then stopped because you were embarrassed or afraid that the other person would laugh at you? That was the devil taking the Word right out of your mouth!

There is nothing that you can do on your own—and nothing that you cannot do with God's help. Like the psalmist, ask God to guard your mouth, so that His truth is always on your lips.

First, get the Word into your heart and mind. Immerse yourself in the truth of the Bible. When you put your whole hope and trust in His Word, then the truth will begin to flow from your mouth, with no effort at all on your part. Declare yourself to be His servant, and He will guide you in everything you say and do.

Father, let nothing but Your
perfect truth flow from my mouth.

Day 44

Nail Down Eternity

44 I will always obey your law,
for ever and ever.

As a believer, you go through three steps on your way to heaven. First, dedicate your heart to obeying the Word of God. Next, continue to study, meditate, and pray upon that Word. Finally, love and obey the Word through all eternity—"for ever and ever."

Your commitment to God doesn't end on Monday morning. It doesn't end when things are going just fine in your life. It doesn't end when you are too tired or discouraged to utter a prayer.

Many popular romantic songs talk about love that lasts "forever and a day" or "until the end of time." The reality is that every earthly relationship will come to an earthly end. It's glorious that the commitment God made to you has no end—and neither does your commitment to Him. A relationship with God is one that is entered into for all eternity.

Lord, I thank You for loving me eternally.
I pledge my eternal love to You.

Day 45

Nail Down the Law

45 I will walk about in freedom,
for I have sought out your precepts.

Have you tried to live strictly according to God's Word? It can be extremeley hard to go more than a few hours or a few days before your attention begins to wander.

Perseverance is a great challenge for the believer. The bondage of sin keeps us from God's path. When the fetters of sin are broken off, then the believer can walk in freedom, never straying from the path of truth. The first step, the psalmist says, is to seek God's precepts.

When you agree to follow a set of laws, you usually agree to give up some of your freedom. Laws of this world restrict your movements and your actions. God's laws are different. They offer the only true freedom: freedom from sin. When you are free from sin, you have no secrets. You need no hiding places. You can walk in complete, abundant, joyful freedom!

Lord, thank You for Your Law, which sets me free!

Day 46

Tough as Nails

46 I will speak of your statutes before
kings and will not be put to shame,

It takes a lot of courage to speak up in front of a king. The Bible proves again and again that men of great holiness become men of great boldness. Reread the story of Nehemiah. Look again at Daniel's courage in Nebuchadnezzar's court. *"The wicked man flees though no one pursues, but the righteous are as bold as a lion"* (Proverbs 28:1).

The psalmist promises God the first act of the threefold service of thanksgiving. In this verse, he promises service with his tongue. He promises to speak up even in the most intimidating circumstances. He knows that there is nothing to be ashamed of when speaking of God's Word.

Have you ever been ashamed of your faith? Do you speak up when someone makes fun of your beliefs? Do you laugh along with others when the Lord's name is taken in vain? Resolve now to face the world with pride: you serve the only living God!

Father, make me bold when I must speak of Your promises, no matter how fearful the situation may seem to me.

Day 47

Hit the Nail on the Heart

⁴⁷ for I delight in your commands because I love them.

This verse describes the second act of the threefold service of thanksgiving, the service of affection.

Why do we follow the laws? Most of us will stop at a red light because we don't want to get hit by a car crossing the intersection, or follow the speed limit to avoid getting a ticket. It is prudent to pay taxes so we won't have to pay big penalties or go to jail. Even though we may follow the laws, few of us spend time reading the legal code. It is hard to imagine a group of people meeting to talk about how much they love the laws of the land!

God's Law is different. When you love God with all your heart, then you take great joy in obeying His laws. It makes you happy to know that you are obeying the God Who loves you. You love His laws because you love Him.

Lord, make obedience to You
the greatest joy of my heart.

Day 48

Nail Down the Truth

⁴⁸ I lift up my hands to your commands, which I love,
and I meditate on your decrees.

This verse shows that serving God engages the whole believer: hand, heart, and head. This is the third act of thanksgiving.

We lift up our hands to show submission to God, or to indicate agreement with God's Word. Hands lifted in prayer are reaching out to God. We lift our hands to God because we love Him.

You are giving your whole heart to Him. Praise, worship, and thanksgiving all flow from a loving heart. Don't you love the Word for its joyous message and for its promise of hope for all eternity? Let the love you feel within express itself in uplifted hands of praise.

In addition to the public expression of uplifted hands, it is important to take private time to enrich your mind with the Word. God commanded us to *"Be still, and know that I am God..."* (Psalm 46:10).

I will serve the Lord my God
with my hands, my heart, and my mind.

CHAPTER SEVEN
Zayin (verses 49-56)

Zayin, Sword of the Lord
(pronounced "zah-yin")

Zayin is shaped like a spear. Hebrew scholars connected weapons and fighting with the struggle for daily existence. The Hebrew word for war is *lacham* and for bread is *lechem*. Swords and other weapons can be used for good: to protect the defenseless, to deter crime, or as a means of judgment.

Reference to "the sword of the Lord," of course, implies the Messiah. *"He made my mouth like a sharpened sword, in the shadow of his hand he hid me; he made me into a polished arrow and concealed me in his quiver"* (Isaiah 49:2). Jesus is the Word, and the Word is a sword which pierces our hearts with its truth.

Psalm 119
Verses 49-56

49 *Remember your word to your servant,*
for you have given me hope.
50 *My comfort in my suffering is this:*
Your promise preserves my life.
51 *The arrogant mock me without restraint,*
but I do not turn from your law.
52 *I remember your ancient laws, O LORD,*
and I find comfort in them.
53 *Indignation grips me because of the wicked,*
who have forsaken your law.
54 *Your decrees are the theme*
of my song wherever I lodge.
55 *In the night I remember your name,*
O LORD, and I will keep your law.
56 *This has been my practice:*
I obey your precepts.

Grab the Promise

The Psalmist's Heart: Comfort in God's Judgment

The psalmist suffers from persecution and affliction, yet he finds great peace in the Law. God's judgment alone is perfect, and the psalmist takes comfort in that fact. He can ignore the ridicule of others, because he has immersed himself in the perfect Word.

God never makes a promise that He does not keep. Hope based on His Word is based on a sure foundation. This is where the psalmist places his hope, and from there he can draw comfort in terrible times.

Your Walk in the Word: Subdue the Enemy

"Take the helmet of salvation and the sword of the Spirit, which is the word of God" (Ephesians 6:17). For Christians, *zayin* is the sword of the Word which comes out of the mouth of Jesus. It was given to you so that you could speak it out of your own mouth and subdue the work of the enemy.

"For the word of God is living and active. Sharper than any double-edged sword, it penetrates even to dividing soul and spirit, joints and marrow; it judges the thoughts and attitudes of the heart" (Hebrews 4:12).

Your Walk in the World: Righteous Judgment

Have you ever wanted to "get even"? Did someone hurt you so much that you wanted to hurt them back? This is a very human, worldly reaction. It is exactly what the enemy wants: to pit people against each other with hate and revenge in their hearts. Don't fall into that snare!

God has given you a wonderful gift: He will take care of all punishments and judgments. This is wonderful because God is a perfect judge. He knows the whole story, and He will judge righteously.

Don't rehearse hurtful events over and over in your head or invent ways to get even. Put God's Word in your mind instead. Soon it will penetrate your heart as well, and you will realize that God alone is capable of giving out righteous judgments. That is not your job. Put thoughts of your enemies out of your mind, and concentrate on the Lord. You will find comfort in Him, if you trust His righteous judgment. *"My soul yearns for you in the night; in the morning my spirit longs for you. When your judgments come upon the earth, the people of the world learn righteousness"* (Isaiah 26:9).

Let God be the judge and jury.

His Gift for You: Comfort

Isn't it glorious that your life is in such capable hands! Be comforted in the thought that He will handle all your problems, if you will just turn them over to Him.

Lord,
Help me to release my desire for revenge against my enemies. I know that You alone are capable of righteous judgment, and so I turn this situation over to You. Thank You for the peace of knowing that You will handle everything according to Your Law. Help me to stop rehearsing these events over and over in my head, and fill me instead with Your love, Your promises, Your freedom.

Amen

DEVOTIONS

Day 49

The Rainbow of Promise

⁴⁹ Remember your word to your servant,
for you have given me hope.

God has never forgotten a single promise to the believer. Throughout the Bible, believers have called on God to remember His promises. Moses reminded God of His promises to the Israelites who were wandering in the desert (Exodus 32:13). Samson asked the Lord to remember him and strengthen him just once more (Judges 16:28). Hannah asked the Lord to remember her by granting her a son (I Samuel 1:11). Job, his life in shambles, begged God to remember him (Job 14:13). Even the thief on the cross asked Jesus to remember him (Luke 23:42).

God enjoys these reminders, because they indicate that His believers have learned and meditated upon His Word. He loves it when you remember Him, and He loves it when you want to be remembered by Him.

Remembrance is so important to God that He even gave us a physical reminder of His promises in the rainbow. *"I have set my rainbow in the clouds, and it will be the sign of the covenant between me and the earth"* (Genesis 9:13).

Remember me, Lord, for I know that You keep all Your promises.

Day 50

The Promise of Comfort

⁵⁰ My comfort in my suffering is this:
Your promise preserves my life.

We cannot live without the promises of God. He has promised us redemption, which we could never earn on our own. He has promised us forgiveness, which we certainly don't deserve. He has even promised us eternal life!

Your life on this earth and your life hereafter both depend on the promises of God. Are you suffering right now—in your finances, your marriage, your health? Seek the comfort that this psalmist had—the comfort that God always remembers you and that He is watching over you always.

How do you know what promises the Lord has stored up especially for you? Open your Bible! All the promises in the Word are for *you!* God laid down His love and concern for you before you were ever born. Nothing is too big for Him to handle. He has promised to take care of you—what more comforting promise could you ask for?

Dear Lord, Your promises are my hope and my refuge!

Day 51

The Promise of Encouraging Words

> 51 *The arrogant mock me without restraint,*
> *but I do not turn from your law.*

The psalmist is beset by scoffers, people making fun of him. Have you ever been hurt by the cruel words of others? Take comfort that their words are insignificant compared to the Word of God. No matter what anyone says about you, they cannot hurt you if you focus on God's encouraging, life-giving Word instead of their mocking words of darkness and destruction.

Even when the words of others make you cry, be thankful for the pain which sends you back to God's arms. Bees sometimes gather the sweetest honey from the bitterest herbs. Christ made the best wine from common water.

Scoffers are acting out of their own pride. They cannot hurt you if your heart is planted firmly in the Word. In fact, you won't even hear them if you focus on the voice of God.

Father, close my ears to the mockery of
the world, and let me hear only You.

Day 52

The Promise of a Righteous Path

52 I remember your ancient laws, O LORD,
and I find comfort in them.

Just as we want God to remember us, God wants us to remember Him. Remember those who became victors through God's workings: Noah, Abraham, David, the entire nation of Israel.

Then, remember how God has worked in your own life. Take time now to thank Him for those miracles, big and little, that He has showered down on you. Don't forget to thank Him for the judgments He has handed down, too. Sometimes He has to rebuke us, to pull out the weeds so that the crops can grow!

This is why His Law is so comforting. He knows much better than we do what is good for us. When He works in your life, even when the direction isn't the one you would have chosen, you can rest in the confidence that He is guiding you down the right path.

Lord, lead me on the path You have chosen for me.

Day 53

The Promise of Salvation

53 Indignation grips me because of the wicked,
who have forsaken your law.

The word *indignation* here can mean a "horror." It is used to describe a pestilential burning wind which the Arabs call *simoon*. Psalm 11:6 says: *"On the wicked he will rain fiery coals and burning sulfur; a scorching wind will be their lot."*

In this verse, the word means "horrible mental distress," like a storm taking over your mind and heart. The psalmist here feels this distress for the wicked. Have you ever mourned for the wicked, godless people around you?

When you know the laws of God, and are living in the joy of His protection, it is especially hard to watch others choosing the way of death.

This is the time to pray for the fallen. Lift up your voice to God and pray that their eyes will be opened to His truth. Your prayers are the most powerful tool you have when your heart is aching for the lost.

Lord, open closed eyes and ears, so that the lost may be saved.

Day 54

The Promise of Protection

⁵⁴ Your decrees are the theme of my song wherever I lodge.

Are your dreams troubled? Do you sleep in peace or is your sleep interrupted with nightmares, worries, anxiety? What you think about at night can affect your dreams as well as your actions in the daytime.

The psalmist meditated upon God's Word at night, no matter where he was. God's presence is available to you every day and every night, no matter what your circumstances. When Jacob was banished and lay all night out in the fields, he found that he was closer to God than he had been in his own tent.

We are all strangers in this world. We can survive only by clinging to the truths that define our real home: the kingdom of God. When you are feeling lost, reach out to your Father, Who will calm you and enfold you with His protection in all situations.

Dear God, let my first thoughts in the morning and my last thoughts at night be of You.

Day 55

The Promise of the Night

⁵⁵ In the night I remember your name, O LORD, and I will keep your law.

Do you praise the Lord in public? Do you sing out at church and pray loudly with your Bible study class? That's wonderful—but it is not enough. The psalmist reminds us here that praise and worship are not just for public display. We also must praise Him in private moments.

When your mind is exhausted with the cares of the world, lie awake and think about Him. The night puts away everything else from your thoughts, and lets your heart be free to commune with the One Whom your soul devoutly loves. You can experience rare seeds of communion with Him in the solitude of night.

When all the voices and instruction of the world have been completely cut off, and your soul is alone with God, this is when He will draw closest to you.

Father, in the quiet of day's end, I long to draw closer to You.

Day 56

The Promise of a Joyful Life

56 This has been my practice: I obey your precepts.

The *zayin* verses deal with the comfort of the Word. The Word will sustain you under affliction, and enable you to survive ridicule. It gives you a tender heart for the worldly and wicked. The Word furnishes songs of hope and comfort in the still, dark night.

All this happiness and comfort can come from only one thing: keeping the statutes of God. When you abide in the will of God, you will find peace and joy unlike anything the world can offer.

Practice is defined as "a customary or habitual performance." When it becomes your practice to obey God's precepts, the Word becomes an inseparable part of you.

Lord, I will make it my practice to read, meditate upon, and obey Your precepts.

CHAPTER EIGHT
Keth (verses 57-64)

Keth, Enclosed, Fenced Area
(pronounced "khet")

Notice how similar the shape of *keth* is to the shape of the fifth letter, *he*. In the case of *he*, the window, there is a small gap near the top. There is no gap in *keth*.

Keth often refers to a fence. Fences are usually built for protection. They may also exist to clearly mark someone's property—to declare, "This is mine," just as God declared Israel to be His: *"But now, this is what the LORD says—he who created you, O Jacob, he who formed you, O Israel: 'fear not, for I have redeemed you; I have summoned you by name; you are mine'"* (Isaiah 43:1).

Psalm 119
Verses 57-64

57 *You are my portion, O LORD;*
I have promised to obey your words.
58 *I have sought your face with all my heart;*
be gracious to me according to your promise.
59 *I have considered my ways*
and have turned my steps to your statutes.
60 *I will hasten and not delay*
to obey your commands.
61 *Though the wicked bind me with ropes,*
I will not forget your law.
62 *At midnight I rise to give you thanks*
for your righteous laws.
63 *I am a friend to all who fear you,*
to all who follow your precepts.
64 *The earth is filled with your love, O LORD;*
teach me your decrees.

A Wall Around—A Fire Within

The Psalmist's Heart: A Sound Believer

Here, the psalmist declares his desire to fellowship with God and to draw closer to Him. The psalmist wants to live within the protective enclosure of God's guidance. He wants to declare to the world that he belongs to God.

These verses describe the eight properties of a sound believer:
- becomes a new creation
- brings forth fruit for God
- earnestly desires God's favor
- wants a Word of grace
- sees own sin and wants to reform
- endures persecution
- doesn't fret and worry
- doesn't rest, but seeks to increase depth of spiritual knowledge

The psalmist loudly and confidently claims his portion as a sound believer and heir of God.

Your Walk in the Word: A Personal Message From God

Everyone has, deep within their hearts, an unnamed longing. That longing is the heart's desire for fellowship with God. Do you remember the eagerness with which you read the Bible when you were newly saved? You were so in love with the Lord that you wanted to know everything about Him!

Do you still approach Scripture with the same eagerness? If not, it's time to renew your relationship with God. The first step is to read His Word. The next step is to hide that Word in your heart; memorize it so it is always with you. The third step is to meditate upon the Word; talk to God about what it means to you.

Choose one scripture which is meaningful to you. Read it over and over and write it on your heart. Then, talk to God about that verse. Listen to what He says to you.

The Bible is a living book. It is constant, yet it is unique to each person who opens it. Open your Bible now, and receive your personal message from God.

Your Walk in the World: To the Victor Go the Spoils

It was the custom in Biblical times for victors in a battle to claim the property of the vanquished. The bravest warriors got first choice of the spoils. They were rewarded with gold, jewels, flocks of sheep, and all sorts of riches.

When you vanquish your old self and become a new creation in the Lord, then you, too, can claim your spoils. Those spoils are the greatest riches of all: fellowship with God.

The Levites took God to be their portion, and left material things to the other tribes. As a new creation, your desire will turn away from material things, too. You will find a greater hunger for the things of God.

His Gift for You: Friendship

What is a "best friend"? A best friend accepts you just as you are. A best friend is there to comfort you, to help you, and to advise you. A best friend listens to all your problems, fears, dreams, and desires. Jesus wants to be your best friend! Invite Him into your life.

Lord,
You are the best friend anyone could have. Thank You for being there for me time after time. Sometimes, I know I didn't even acknowledge Your presence, but still You were there, watching over me. I'd like to be a good friend to You, too. I want to spend time with You and learn everything I can about You. I want to walk with You for the rest of my life, and live with You in rejoicing and praise for all eternity.

Amen

DEVOTIONS

Day 57

A Wall Against Temptation

⁵⁷ You are my portion, O LORD;
I have promised to obey your words.

Martin Luther counseled every Christian to answer all temptation with the words, "I am a Christian." No matter what Satan brings to you, you will be safe if you answer, "I am a Christian; the Lord is my portion."

When Satan came to Eve with the apple, what a difference it would have made if she had answered, "I don't need that apple! The *Lord* is my portion." When Noah was tempted by wine, what a difference it would have made if he had simply said, "The Lord is my portion" (Genesis 9:20-25).

What a difference Moses made when, instead of taking the crown of Egypt, he said, "The Lord is my portion." When David was a fugitive, living in caves, he was satisfied, because he took the Lord for his portion.

How do you answer the temptations of the world? Do you lust after money, fame, and popularity? Discover the peace and joy of taking the Lord as your portion!

Lord, I want to be satisfied with You as my generous portion!

Day 58

A Wall of Prayer

⁵⁸   I have sought your face with all my heart;
be gracious to me according to your promise.

Prayer is the heart at work. God hears your heart without your mouth, but He never hears your mouth without your heart.

When you pray with all your heart, you are concentrating with your intellect, your will, and your emotions. God deserves nothing less. When you are seeking the face of God with all your heart, you will discover yourself doing these things:

- praying often, always
- searching the Word
- seeking the advice of more mature Christians

God has offered you commandments, directions, and promises. The promises are very important: they are the food of faith. God has promised you mercy. When you seek Him with all your heart, He will not, He *cannot,* deny you!

I seek You with all my mind and heart and soul.
Be gracious to me, Lord.

Day 59

A Wall of Self-Examination

[59] *I have considered my ways and have*
turned my steps to your statutes.

When we get in touch with the Word, it becomes our mirror. Do you have the courage to look at your reflection in the mirror of the Word? We frequently avoid looking directly into that glass because we are afraid of what we might see.

Do you worry about what other people will think about your new haircut? Do you clean your house for company? Why are we so concerned with what other people think? Their judgment is of the world. The only thing against which we should be measuring ourselves is the standard of the Word.

The psalmist considers only God's Word. *Considered* here means "thinking accurately, seriously, studiously, and curiously." Do you bring all these attributes to your meditations on the Word?

Father, help me to measure myself
only against Your standards.

Day 60

A Wall Against Procrastination

⁶⁰ I will hasten and not delay to obey your commands.

Are you a procrastinator? Do you put off until tomorrow the things you should be doing today? Do you intend to start attending church regularly...next month? Are you going to start that Bible Study class...as soon as you can find the time?

Procrastination is the tool of the enemy. He uses it to keep you away from God. When you make plans to do what God wants you to do, Satan whispers in your ear, "You can always do that later." Don't listen to him!

Disobedience to the Word can come about through direct actions, but just as often, it comes from delay. Procrastinating in your service to God is not only disgraceful; it is dangerous.

Have you been putting off something God has asked you to do? Don't delay another moment! Obedience to God is not something you do in your spare time. It is the most urgent matter on your "To Do" list. Do it now!

God, grant me a sense of urgency in pursuing
Your purpose for my life.

Day 61

A Wall of Remembrance

⁶¹ Though the wicked bind me with ropes,
I will not forget your law.

Binding with ropes refers to any kind of oppression. God's people have experienced oppression by the wicked in almost every age. Pharaoh sought to keep the Jews in slavery. Saul sought to destroy David. Jesus was persecuted by the very people He came to save.

In times of oppression, it can be especially hard to trust God's Word, yet that is the very time when His Law is most precious.

Are you feeling oppressed? Are you *bound up with ropes* of worldliness? This is the time to turn to God. He is your only hope for deliverance. He is just waiting for you to ask Him. Remember His Word, and you will be freed from the oppressors of the world.

Lord, in my oppression, I am clinging to
Your promise of deliverance in Your Word.

Day 62

A Wall of Thanksgiving

62   At midnight I rise to give you thanks for your righteous laws.

It is usually easy to give thanks when things are going well. We know that things were not going well for this psalmist. In the last verse, the wicked had bound him with ropes. Doesn't it seem strange to be thanking God for such awful circumstances?

The world is darkest at midnight. Yet this is the time that the psalmist rises up with thanksgiving! What is his secret? He knows God's Word, and God's promises to those who trust in Him. Even when defeat seems inevitable, He knows that God has promised victory.

When your world is darkest, you can trust the Lord. Call out to Him to calm your spirit with His faithfulness. Trust in Him all the time, in good times and bad. He will not forsake you.

Dear God, l lift my heart with thanksgiving
for Your faithfulness to me.

Day 63

A Wall Against Bad Company

63   I am a friend to all who fear you,
to all who follow your precepts.

With whom do you spend your time? Are your friends also friends of God? It is true that we tend to become like the people with whom we associate. The psalmist cautions you to welcome the people of God. Spend your time with them. Shun the company that shuns God.

If you really love God, then you will be drawn to others who love Him. Beware of the voice of the enemy suggesting that you won't have any friends if you stop hanging out with your ungodly associates.

You are never alone when your best friend is Jesus! If you pursue His Word and His Will, then godly people will be drawn to you. They will help you grow, and you will help them grow.

Jesus, thank You for being my best Friend.
Help me to be a friend to Your people.

Day 64

A Wall of Mercy

⁶⁴ *The earth is filled with your love,*
O LORD; teach me your decrees.

God's love is manifested to us in two wonderful ways: in nature and in His Word. His love is reflected on the earth in His glorious creation. Everything exists because of His love. Nothing has life without His love. His creations are obvious to anyone who looks, even to unbelievers.

The revelation of God's love in the Word is much more difficult to discover. It takes time, effort, and sacrifice on your part, just as your salvation came only with Jesus' great effort and sacrifice.

Understanding of the Word is a gift that can be granted only by God, and it is a gift that must be requested. The psalmist asks God for this understanding again and again. Every time you open your Bible, ask God to open your eyes to His message of mercy.

Merciful Lord, reveal Your Word to me
that I might receive Your mercies.

CHAPTER NINE
Teth (verses 65-72)

Teth, the Serpent
(pronounced "tet")

Hebrew scholars associate *teth* with "mud." It is symbolic of physical matter. Man was created out of mud by God's hand, and the physical body will return to the earth.

The shape of *teth* suggests a serpent. The serpent, of course, was the tempter in the Garden of Eden. It is something coiled back upon itself, something twisted up. The serpent is venomous and deadly.

The evil of the serpent can be contrasted with the goodness of our Lord. It serves to remind us of the protection and mercies of Jesus. *"The Lord is gracious, and full of compassion; slow to anger, and of great mercy. The Lord is good to all: and his tender mercies are over all his works"* (Psalm 145:8,9 KJV).

Psalm 119
Verses 65-72

65 *Do good to your servant*
according to your word, O LORD.
66 *Teach me knowledge and good judgment,*
for I believe in your commands.
67 *Before I was afflicted I went astray,*
but now I obey your word.
68 *You are good, and what you do is good;*
teach me your decrees.
69 *Though the arrogant*
have smeared me with lies,
I keep your precepts with all my heart.
70 *Their hearts are callous and unfeeling,*
but I delight in your law.
71 *It was good for me to be afflicted*
so that I might learn your decrees.
72 *The law from your mouth is*
more precious to me
than thousands of pieces of silver and gold.

Trouble Knocks Twice

The Psalmist's Heart: Thanks for Afflictions

These verses deal with affliction. Men have forged lies against the psalmist. He is surrounded by callous and unfeeling people, yet he is grateful for this affliction. Why? Because, before he was afflicted, he had wandered from the Word. The trials and troubles sent him running back to the Word.

The sting of the serpent can cause us to circle back to the place where we belong. Isn't it wonderful how God uses pain and problems to cleanse us and encourage us? Affliction is beneficial to the trusting and obedient soul. Affliction breaks and embitters the rebellious person, but it heals and ennobles the obedient.

Your Walk in the Word: The Rewards of Adversity

This octave is a witness of life experience, allowing us to see how God makes excellent use of adversity. The Word is fulfilled in our experiences. They testify to the goodness of God, the graciousness of His dealings with us, and the preciousness of His Word.

Painful experiences are especially rewarding, because they endear the scriptures to us. They make us love the Lord of the Word. Isn't it wonderful to be a laborer for the Lord? He gives us really light work, a lot of maintenance, tremendous encouragement, and liberal wages.

Rejoice that He has called you to do His work. Rejoice especially in the face of affliction. Rejoice when His love is all you have. Rejoice with the psalmist that God's Word is more enduring than the troubles of the material world.

Your Walk in the World: What's Really Important to You?

Who is more important to you, your friends or Jesus? What do you value more, your bank account or your Bible? Would you give up your life for the Lord?

John Mason said, "God's Word has to be nearer to us than our friends, dearer to us than our lives, sweeter to us than our liberty, and pleasanter to us than all earthly comforts." Is the Word this important to you?

Martin Luther said that he wouldn't want to live in heaven without the Word, and with the Word, he could live well enough in hell. This might be a bit extreme, but God's Word is mighty and powerful. It will see you through any troubles that the world serves up, and it is more valuable than any treasure the world might offer.

His Gift for You: Life Experiences

How wisely God leads us along our life paths! He gives us experiences we might not choose for ourselves, but every experience contributes to our spiritual walk.

Father,
Thank You for experiences, good and bad, which teach me more about trusting You. Don't let adversity make me bitter, but teach me the lessons that I need to learn. Guide me on this path, and hold my feet steady so that I do not stumble against the rocks which the world throws up to defeat me. I praise the name of the God Who loves me and showers His mercies down on me.

Amen

DEVOTIONS

PSALM 119

TETH
the Serpent

MEDITATIONS

Day 65

The Trouble With Servants

⁶⁵ *Do good to your servant according to your word, O LORD.*

The psalmist establishes himself as the servant and God as his master. God is a good master. He demands very little of us. He offers us mercy, love, and righteous laws. He pays the ultimate wages: eternal life.

Yet, as good as our master is to us, we often complain and whine when things don't go the way we want. Take your lesson from the ultimate servant: Jesus. Though He was worthy to be served, He chose to serve, instead. Paul says that Jesus made Himself "nothing," an obedient servant: *"...but made himself nothing, taking the very nature of a servant, being made in human likeness. And being found in appearance as a man, he humbled himself and became obedient to death—even death on a cross!"* (Philippians 2:7,8).

Do you seek ways to serve, or do you seek to be served? Commit yourself now to serve as Christ did.

Lord, I want to serve You.
Help me to see where my services are needed.

Day 66

The Trouble With Gossip

⁶⁶ *Teach me knowledge and good judgment,*
for I believe in your commands.

When your heart is right, your head will be made right. If you seek God's truth, He will teach you. The first step is believing and trusting His commandments. Then God will grant you knowledge and good judgment.

What constitutes "good judgment"?

- It discriminates between truth and error.
- It avoids the curious and the speculative.
- It knows that good food may, under some circumstances, be poisonous. Therefore it is careful in its use of truths.

Do you always use good judgment when you are talking to your friends? Are you careful to always discriminate between truth and error? Do you consider that even the truth can harm someone if it is used wrongly? Have you ever been guilty of gossiping about someone? Before you open your mouth, let God be your censor. Ask Him to impose His good judgment on all your words.

Lord, guard my tongue, and let me show Your good judgment in everything I say.

Day 67

The Trouble With Prosperity

67 *Before I was afflicted I went astray, but now I obey your word.*

Often, trials act as a hedge of thorns to keep us in good pasture, and prosperity can be a gap through which we go astray. The trials usually send us running back to His loving arms, begging for His protection and mercy.

Have you experienced times when everything was going right? The bills were paid, the kids were behaving, your health was good, and your marriage was strong. Be very, very careful in such times. When the world is treating us well, we often neglect the Lord. It seems that we frequently turn God's abundance into an occasion for sin.

Remember to thank Him and stay close to Him during good times!

Father, I thank You for all experiences, good and bad, which teach me more about You.

Day 68

The Trouble With Experience

68 *You are good, and what you do is good; teach me your decrees.*

Has an unbeliever ever asked you, "Why, if God is so good, do such bad things happen in this world?" Of course, God doesn't create the bad things; everything He does is good. The real proof of God's mercy is that

He saves us from having as many bad experiences as we actually deserve.

Because of His nature, God can use evil things to bring about good. The psalmist reminds us here that even bad things in our lives can be used by God for good. Jesus faced one of the worst possible experiences: humiliation and death on the cross. What a wonderful result came out of that terrible experience!

Lift up your praise to God for all the goodness He showers down on you. Ask Him to use all of your experiences to prepare your heart for His great and good gifts.

Lord, thank You that You are good,
and that everything You do is good.

Day 69

The Trouble With Pride

69 Though the arrogant have smeared me with lies,
I keep your precepts with all my heart.

Pride in yourself, or in any of your accomplishments, is a falsehood. Everything we accomplish is done with the help and blessing of God, so it is dishonest to take credit for it. The lie is in believing that we have any power outside of God's love. Proud men must, by their very nature, lie.

Satan has two arms with which he wrestles against us: lies and violence. He uses both of them very well. When Satan attacks you with slander or physical ailments, the best solution is complete obedience to the Word.

Turn to God. Ask Him to defend you against the attacks of the enemy. Remember Jesus' example. When He was slandered and tortured, He refused to defend Himself. Instead, He asked the Father to forgive His enemies.

When you are being attacked, respond with obedience to God. Forgive your attackers. Pray for them.

Father, I look to You to defend me when I am attacked.
I put all my hope in You.

Day 70

The Trouble With Heart Disease

70 Their hearts are callous and unfeeling, but I delight in your law.

Arrogant, prideful people have a serious disease of the heart. Their hearts are turned only to themselves. People with this disease take no delight in God. They ignore His Law. They dislike God's people. They lie easily to themselves, and to others. This is a terminal disease; it inevitably leads to death.

There is an inoculation against this disease! It is found in the Word of God. God's truth will overcome the lies of the arrogant. The heart that turns to God will be healed. The heart that delights in God's Law is so healthy that it is assured of living forever!

Search your own heart for selfishness and pride. Guard against becoming callous and unfeeling. Meditate upon the beautiful Word of God. Fill your heart with it. Inoculate it against the disease of arrogance.

Dear God, cleanse my heart, and fill it with Your love and mercy.

Day 71

The Trouble With Trouble

71 It was good for me to be afflicted so that I might learn your decrees.

Just as waters are purest when they're in motion, saints are usually holiest when they're in affliction. The purest gold is the most pliable. Trouble brings experience, and experience brings wisdom.

By the time Jonah came up from the depths of the ocean, he had learned a lot from God. He was also open to learning more, so God dealt with him concerning the worm, the wind, and the wilted gourd (Jonah 4:5-11).

Sometimes a naughty child won't listen to the rules until he has suffered the consequences: the time out or the spanking. It is only after the punishment that the rebellious child is prepared to listen to his parents' teaching.

Are you just like that rebellious child? Ask God to use your afflictions to teach you. Let your troubles open your heart to His Word.

Jesus, thank You, because even afflictions make
me receptive to Your teaching.

Day 72

The Trouble With Treasure

⁷² The law from your mouth is more precious to me
than thousands of pieces of silver and gold.

Merchants like to place a value on their merchandise, estimating the price that someone might pay in order to own it. What price can be put on God's Word? How can you compare it to gold and silver?

- Without the Word, gold and silver may be a curse.
- Gold and silver have to be sold in order to be worth anything. The Word yields its treasures freely, over and over.
- No matter where you hide your gold, someone may steal it. The Word cannot be stolen, once it is hidden in your heart.
- Gold and silver do not change you, but the Word refines and improves you.
- Gold and silver cannot extend your life by a single day, but the Word gives eternal life.

Which treasure would you rather have? *"For where your treasure is, there your heart will be also"* (Matthew 6:21). Lay up the priceless treasure of the Word in your heart.

Dear Father, my heart yearns for the priceless
treasure of the Words of Your mouth.

CHAPTER TEN
Jod (verses 73-80)

PSALM 119
JOD
the Open
Hand
MEDITATIONS

Jod, the Open Hand
(pronounced "yode")

Jod is the smallest letter in the Hebrew alphabet. It is not much bigger than a comma. Jesus spoke of the letter *jod* in Matthew 5:18. Today, we refer to this letter when we say we are going to "jot down a few words."

An open hand can denote power, possession, and ownership. It also has the power to bless others, or the ability to be generous. Most often, *jod* is the right hand.

Just as the hand is essential to a human being, *jod* is essential in the Hebrew alphabet. It begins some of the most important words, including the Hebrew words for Jehovah, Jesus, salvation, and Jerusalem.

As the tenth letter in the Hebrew alphabet, *jod* also brings to mind our own ten fingers, and the Ten Commandments. This comparison has led some scholars to associate *jod* with two open hands—hands which can hold the open Bible.

Best of all, *jod* represents Jesus—the open hands of God, generously blessing each one of us.

Psalm 119
Verses 73-80

73   *Your hands made me and formed me;*
give me understanding to
learn your commands.
74   *May those who fear you rejoice when*
they see me,
for I have put my hope in your word.
75 *I know, O LORD, that your laws are righteous,*
and in faithfulness you have afflicted me.
76   *May your unfailing love be my comfort,*
according to your promise to your servant.
77   *Let your compassion come to me*
that I may live,
for your law is my delight.
78   *May the arrogant be put to shame for*
wronging me without cause;
but I will meditate on your precepts.
79   *May those who fear you turn to me,*
those who understand your statutes.
80*May my heart be blameless toward your decrees,*
that I may not be put to shame.

The Power of the Hand

The Psalmist's Heart: A Prayer to His Creator

The psalmist is reflecting on his own personal experiences here. He is deep in sorrow, but hopes and expects that God will deliver him. He then hopes to be made a blessing to others.

He recognizes that he has been created by God's hands. One of the greatest reasons for abandoning our lives to the rule of God is that He is the one Who has made us. That is why His laws are perfect for us.

The psalmist knows that the judgments of Jehovah are righteous, and that his affliction is part of God's faithfulness.

Your Walk in the Word: Your Owner's Manual

When you buy a new appliance, there is usually an owner's manual packaged with it, which tells you how to operate the appliance and keep it in good working order. If you have a problem with the appliance, you are more likely to receive accurate trouble-shooting information from the manual than from a friend, coworker, or stranger on the street.

Your manufacturer has given you an owner's manual. It contains the most accurate information on how you function, and on the care required to keep you in good working order. That manual is the *Holy Bible*.

The laws God has set down for your life really work—because they were written by your maker. Read your owner's manual for the very best advice on living a healthy, righteous, and rewarding life.

Your Walk in the World: How Do You Use Your Hands?

Throughout His ministry, Jesus used His hands dramatically. He healed most often by touch—reaching out with loving hands to cure all sorts of physical disease, from blindness to leprosy to paralysis. Jesus' hands broke the bread that fed thousands (Matthew 14:19-21). When Peter began to sink in the waves, Jesus reached out His hand (Matthew 14:31).

Jesus also used His hands to rebuke. He made a whip of cords, and used it to drive the merchants out of the temple. His hands were healing hands, and they were correcting hands. In every way, they were loving hands.

How do you use your hands? There are so many ways that Christians can use their hands to be a blessing to the world:
- to give a gentle touch for one who is suffering
- to prepare food, drink, and gifts for the needy
- to write a note or dial the phone to contact someone who is lonely
- to teach young people right from wrong
- to lift in praise and worship

His Gift for You: Correction

Hands can be used to bless and they can be used to rebuke. While we are usually grateful to God when He hands down blessings, it is important to recognize the benefit of His corrections, too. We need to praise Him for pointing out our shortcomings and lifting us above them.

Lord,
As much as I thank You for the blessings You have bestowed upon me, I am even more grateful for the corrections that You make in my life. As my creator, You know exactly what is best for me. Help me to stop trying to operate by myself out of my own ignorance. I would rather be guided by Your wisdom, Your love, and Your righteousness.

Amen

DEVOTIONS

JOD
the Open
Hand

MEDITATIONS

Day 73

The Power of Education

> 73 *Your hands made me and formed me;*
> *give me understanding to learn your commands.*

When we study the human body, we are amazed at the marvelous skill the Lord used in its formation. If He is this concerned with our physical creation, then certainly He is just as concerned about our spiritual creation. He is prepared to put forth great effort until our souls perfectly bear His image.

The Lord Who made us, also makes us learn. Just as our physical body must grow and develop, so must our minds and hearts. God knows best what each of us needs to learn. The one Who gives us power to stand, also gives us grace to understand.

Educators today like to talk about "individualizing" learning programs in schools. God was the inventor of the individualized learning plan! He has planned our lives to be filled with exactly what we need in order to learn and grow. Put your learning plan in the hands of your creator!

Lord, thank You for teaching me what I need to learn.
Please make me an eager student.

Day 74

The Power of a Joyful Attitude

> 74 *May those who fear you rejoice when they see me,*
> *for I have put my hope in your word.*

When a man of God gets grace for himself, then he becomes a blessing to others. Hopeful men bring gladness wherever they go.

What do you bring to your friends and family? Do you remind them of all the bad things that have happened or are likely to happen? Do you give them a catalog of your aches and pains? If your conversations are full of complaints, worries, and problems, then you are not testifying for God; you are testifying for Satan.

Your attitude alone can be a testimony to the gifts of God. You have been forgiven! You are assured of eternal life! Considering the magnitude of these gifts, what do you have to complain about? Reflect your joy and gratitude in every situation, and you will be a blessing to your friends and family—and most of all to God!

Lord, let me be a reflection of Your grace and
love in all my relationships.

Day 75

The Power of Chastening

75 *I know, O LORD, that your laws are righteous,*
and in faithfulness you have afflicted me.

It is so easy to love and thank God for His many blessings. Do you love His chastening, too? That seems to take a higher degree of faith.

Believe it or not, afflictions can add to our happiness. Is this hard to understand? When a parent warns a child not to touch a hot stove, the child might ignore the advice. In that case, it takes a burn to convince the child of the danger. No parent wants to see a child hurt, but what if that little burn on the finger will prevent a future tragedy?

God's judgments help us discern between good and evil. "*...The Sovereign LORD will wipe away the tears from all faces...*" (Isaiah 25:8). Your tears will be turned into joy. The horrible agony of the Cross was preparation for salvation.

All of God's judgments are for our happiness.

Father, help me to look up to You
in low times as well as in high times.

Day 76

The Power of Friendship

*76   May your unfailing love be my comfort,
according to your promise to your servant.*

The Hebrew word for *unfailing* love also means "befriending." We are told in Exodus 33:11, *"The LORD would speak to Moses face to face, as a man speaks with his friend..."* Jesus frequently addressed people as "friend." Jesus called Lazarus His friend, and He was Himself also called a "friend of tax collectors and sinners." He even called Judas "friend" at the very moment Judas betrayed Him!

What do you look for in a friend? Even casual acquaintances can share your happy times. It takes a true friend to comfort you in times of trouble. It takes a true friend to stick with you even when you have done something terrible. Jesus is that kind of friend.

Comfort is a promise and gift from your friend, Jesus. You can take comfort in His love, which never fails. He loves you no matter what you have done. You can take comfort in the knowledge that He loved you enough to die for you. You can take comfort that He has promised you eternal life, and He always keeps His promises!

Dear Lord, it is wonderful that You are not only my creator, my savior, and my king, but You are also my unfailing friend.

Day 77

The Power of Compassion

*77   Let your compassion come to me that I may live,
for your law is my delight.*

Why has God blessed you? Why did Jesus die for you? Was it because you deserved it? No, of course not! Not one of us is good enough to "earn" salvation.

There is one simple reason that God has blessed you: He is a merciful and compassionate God. He loves you. It is that simple.

The psalmist acknowledges that his very life is dependent upon God's compassion, and he takes great delight in that. God is pleased to extend His grace to you. Do you take the same delight in extending mercy and compassion to others? It is not enough to do good deeds. If you are to follow in Jesus' footsteps, you must *enjoy* being merciful.

Indeed, the more mercy you display to others, the more you can claim for yourself. Jesus said, *"Blessed are the merciful, for they will be shown mercy"* (Matthew 5:7). Search your heart now. Do you delight in showing compassion to those around you?

Father, give me a compassionate and merciful heart.

Day 78

The Power of God's Armor

78 *May the arrogant be put to shame for wronging me without cause; but I will meditate on your precepts.*

When Satan stirs up his instruments to hate those whom the Lord loves, the Lord stirs up His power to help and defend them. Why does Satan so often use the arrogant as his instruments? It is because the arrogant think that they don't need God. They refuse to be subject to Him. These are the same people who then become angry with the people of God.

Look at Pharaoh, who said, *"...Who is the LORD, that I should obey him and let Israel go? I do not know the LORD and I will not let Israel go"* (Exodus 5:2).

The enemy fights with the weapons of the flesh: wickedness and falsehood. God's people will fight back with the Spirit. Do you meet wickedness with wickedness, or do you meet wickedness with the Word? Do you answer falsehood with falsehoods, or do you answer falsehoods with the Word?

Dear God, when I am under attack by the arrogant, grant me Your armor to protect me.

Day 79

The Power of Reconciliation

79 *May those who fear you turn to me, those who understand your statutes.*

Zeal for God's Law brings people together. Just as believers are indignant when they see arrogant people reject God, they are drawn to those who share a love for God's Word.

The Body of Christ consists of all who love God, joined together in unity. Love for God brought Jacob and Laban back together (Genesis 31:24-59). That reconciliation resulted in the farewell that people of God frequently repeat to each other upon parting: "...*May the LORD keep watch between you and me when we are away from each other*" (Genesis 31:49). Later, God reconciled Jacob and Esau.

God can make the hearts of others turn to you. He can give you peace with your enemies. First, you must seek understanding of His statutes, and love God with all your heart. God will handle the rest.

Father, I place my troubled relationships in Your hands.

Day 80

The Power of Trust

[80] *May my heart be blameless toward your decrees,*
that I may not be put to shame.

The psalmist wants a perfect heart. Why? Because anything less than perfection would make him ashamed. The greatest shame for a believer is to live a life of hypocrisy.

Each of the last five verses have each contained a request:
- for comfort
- for life
- for vindication
- for the power of witness
- for perfection

None of these things can be acquired on your own. You must trust God for each one. If your trust is totally in God, and not in yourself, then you will be free of the shame of hypocrisy.

Search your heart now for areas in which you may be trusting yourself instead of God. Turn them all over to God.

Dear Father, help me trust You to provide all that I
need in this life and forever.

CHAPTER ELEVEN
Kaph (verses 81-88)

PSALM 119 KAPH Palm of the Hand MEDITATIONS

Kaph, Palm of the Hand
(pronounced "kawf")

Kaph describes the palm of the hand when used as a container, and refers to the measure held in a cupped palm. Just as *jod* shows the hand as power, *kaph* shows the hand as productivity and accomplishment.

Kaph can also mean "bent." The Hebrew word for wing is *kanaph*. It is easy to see the similarity between our hands and the wings of a bird. Much of human efficiency involves the hands at work; the greatest part of a bird's efficiency involves his wings at work.

The hand of God protects man, God carries us on His wings (Exodus 19:4; Deuteronomy 32:11,12), and we take refuge under His wings (Ruth 2:12; Psalms 17:8; 57:1; 61:4; 91:4). There is healing in His wings: *"But unto you that fear my name shall the Sun of righteousness arise with healing in his wings..."* (Malachi 4:2 KJV).

Psalm 119
Verses 81-88

81 *My soul faints with longing for your salvation,
but I have put my hope in your word.*

82 *My eyes fail, looking for your promise;
I say, "When will you comfort me?"*

83 *Though I am like a wineskin in the smoke,
I do not forget your decrees.*

84 *How long must your servant wait?
When will you punish my persecutors?*

85 *The arrogant dig pitfalls for me,
contrary to your law.*

86 *All your commands are trustworthy;
help me, for men persecute me without cause.*

87 *They almost wiped me from the earth,
but I have not forsaken your precepts.*

88 *Preserve my life according to your love,
and I will obey the statutes of your mouth.*

Stars Come Out at Midnight

The Psalmist's Heart: A Balm for Your Sorrows

This psalm deals with sorrow, and discusses the wonderful confidence which comes from loving and trusting God. No matter how dark the circumstances around you, trust in God provides light for your way.

The psalmist's soul faints; his eyes fail. Men have wrongfully used him, but he has not forgotten God's precepts. His soul clings to the will of God. He places unshaken confidence in God's divine loving-kindness, even in the darkest of nights.

Your Walk in the Word: For the Midnights of Your Life

These verses are sometimes called the "midnight" of Psalm 119. Have you ever experienced a "midnight" in your life? Such times are dark; you are filled with anguish and depression. These are the times when you absolutely must place all your hope in the grace of God. Hope in Him can keep your soul from fainting. Hope gives you the smelling salts of God's promise.

In the midnights of your life, turn your eyes upwards, with faith in Him. When there is no one else to comfort you, He is there. Let Him hold you in His hands, and you will begin to see the twinkling stars of His righteousness. Before long, you will glimpse the first light of dawn.

Your Walk in the World: Receiving Hands, Giving Hands

The bent hand, symbolic of *kaph*, can represent either the hand of a giver or the hand of a receiver. You are the receiver of the many blessings of God. Think of your cupped hand held out, receiving all those wondrous gifts!

Your hands are also designed to give. If you are living in His image, then you will not only be a receiver, you will also be a giver. Are there any hands reaching out to you? Look around you. There are many who need what you have to give. When you give gifts of money and material things, you are sharing the bounty which God bestowed on you. You can also share gifts of the Spirit in the same way.

Someone is discouraged and could use a pat on the back. Someone is lonely and could use a friend. Someone needs a ride to church or could use a couple of hours of baby-sitting. Reach out with giving hands. You will be amazed at how your own blessings multiply!

His Gift for You: Faithfulness

The hands of God are:

• protective

- permanent
- innocent
- skillful
- essential
- faithful
- pierced for your sake

The hands of God are always ready to protect and bless you. They were even pierced in order to save you. His strong wings will lift you up, and shelter you in times of trouble. Trust those wonderful hands!

Father,
In the storms of life, You shelter me in the wings of Your mercy. You shower me with blessings and hold me safe in Your strong hands. I can trust You to be righteous and just, no matter what the world's judgments may be. I am so grateful for Your faithfulness, which makes stars shine in my heart on the darkest night.

Amen

DEVOTIONS

Day 81

A Star for the Lost

81   My soul faints with longing for your salvation,
but I have put my hope in your word.

Fainting is usually a physical reaction, but here, the psalmist's very soul faints! A body may faint for lack of food or air or rest. The soul of the psalmist faints with a desire for the salvation of the Lord. Day-to-day living is enough to make Christians faint with a desire for the world to be saved. Just reading a daily newspaper is enough to make us weep for this lost world. The only hope is in the gospel, God's promise for the entire world.

Today is your day to carry that hope to a fainting world. Speak to a friend, neighbor, or family member about Jesus. Write a check, along with an encouraging note, to a missionary. Resolve to pray daily for your church's outreach program.

Lord, show me how to share Your promise with a lost world.

Day 82

A Star for the Hopeless

82   My eyes fail, looking for your promise;
I say, "When will you comfort me?"

Sometimes we have to believe even when there is no apparent evidence of God's faithfulness. Sometimes, we have to believe in His light when there is no visible moonlight or starlight. *"Though he slay me, yet will I hope in him..."* (Job 13:15).

Have you ever felt hopeless? Have you been trapped in a situation with no obvious way out? Those are the times to cry out to God for help.

Of course, in certain situations you want help *right now*, and, sometimes, help doesn't come immediately. The hardest part may be waiting for God's timing. The same spirit of faith that teaches a man to cry earnestly also teaches him to wait patiently.

Look again at the promise in God's Word. You will find that mercy is in the Lord's hand. It will come forth in His time.

Father, I give thanks that You are with me even when my eyes fail.

Day 83

A Star for Doubters

83 *Though I am like a wineskin in the smoke,*
I do not forget your decrees.

Skins used to hold wine were hung on the walls of the tents. With cooking and heating fires, those tents got really smoky, and the wineskins became black and sooty. The heat of the fires would wrinkle the skins, and crack them.

Sorrow can make you feel dark and dismal. Your mind can be parched by persecution and mental suffering. As the smoke of discouragement surrounds you, you may feel as useless as those cracked, dried up wineskins.

When times are black and hot, put your hope in God. Never give up on the truth that is outside those smoky doubts. When you remember God's promises, the fire cannot consume your faith; the smoke cannot smother it. Even though your eyes are tormented with smoke, cry out to God for His delivering hand.

Dear God, stay with me through the suffocating smoke of doubt.
Help me to trust in You.

Day 84

A Star for Patience

84 *How long must your servant wait?*
When will you punish my persecutors?

Many prayers are not answered immediately. One of the hardest jobs of a believer is waiting for God. Sometimes, it seems like a long, long time between your request and His answer.

The Bible is full of instructions on waiting for God. They tell us when to wait, how to wait, and why to wait. Here are some of my favorites:

"*Be still before the LORD and wait patiently for him; do not fret when men succeed in their ways, when they carry out their wicked schemes*" (Psalm 37:7).

"*Do not say, 'I'll pay you back for this wrong!' Wait for the LORD, and he will deliver you*" (Proverbs 20:22).

"*It is good to wait quietly for the salvation of the LORD*" (Lamentations 3:26).

"*'Therefore wait for me,' declares the LORD*" (Zephaniah 3:8).

"*Keep yourselves in God's love as you wait for the mercy of our Lord Jesus Christ to bring you to eternal life*" (Jude 21).

Father, grant me the patience to wait for You.

Day 85

A Star in the Pit

[85] *The arrogant dig pitfalls for me,*
contrary to your law.

It is interesting that in the Bible, time and time again, the people who dug the pits were the ones who fell into them. Absalom dug pits for David, but in the end he was dumped into a pit (II Samuel 18:17). Joseph was placed in a pit by his brothers, but they were the ones who ended up in the pit of famine and starvation (Genesis 37-42).

Four times in Psalms, we are told of the follies of those who set traps for others. The first is Psalm 7:15: "*He who digs a hole and scoops it out falls into the pit he has made.*" The same message is repeated in Psalms 9:15, 35:8, and 57:6.

Proverbs 26:27 contains this warning: "*If a man digs a pit, he will fall into it; if a man rolls a stone, it will roll back on him.*" This warning is repeated in Ecclesiastes 10:8.

Be sure that you are not digging any pits with gossip, criticism, or efforts at revenge. You might find yourself at the bottom of your own pit!

Dear Lord, show me whether I am
digging any pits in my relationships.

Day 86

A Star for the Inner Life

86   All your commands are trustworthy;
help me, for men persecute me without cause.

"Help me, Lord" is a golden prayer. It is as precious as it is short. The words may be few, but the meaning is full. On earth, the psalmist may be persecuted, but he has an eternal comfort that cannot be touched.

No matter how severe his afflictions, the psalmist stays true to God's commands. If you stick to the *precepts* of the Word, you will be rescued by the *promises* of the Word. The psalmist says he would rather die than forsake the Lord. Can you say the same thing?

If so, you will not die, but will live to see the overthrow of those who hate God. When your inner life is vigorous, everything else will be resolved. Pray with a sound heart—a heart filled with the Word.

Lord, do a heart work in me, so that my heart may be right with You.

Day 87

A Star for the Child of God

87   They almost wiped me from the earth,
but I have not forsaken your precepts.

You can feel the weight of terrible afflictions in these last few verses. The psalmist's enemies are trying to destroy him, and they have almost succeeded.

Almost is the key word here. People who do not know God cannot understand the power of faith. It is impossible to completely destroy a believer!

How strong is your faith? Can you withstand worldly attacks like the psalmist, and still hold onto your belief in God? It is a temptation to abandon His precepts when things are going badly. When under attack, it is natural to seek revenge, to attack, or even resort to violence. This is exactly what the enemy hopes you will do.

Your best weapon against these assaults is the Word which is stored in your heart. Cling to His promises even in the worst of times, and He will not fail you. You are His child for all eternity. No one can take you out of His hands.

Father, hold me close and protect Your child when the enemy attacks.

Day 88

A Star of Glory

⁸⁸ Preserve my life according to your love,
and I will obey the statutes of your mouth.

The surest evidence of God's love is His good work in you. Are you the same person you were before you were saved? Of course not! Once you invited Jesus into your heart, He began to work on you. His life is in you, and you become more like Him each day.

In this way, a continuous circle is established. As He changes you, and you discover the joy of following Him, you become more obedient to Him. Your increased obedience then increases His ability to work in you. This process continues until you emerge in His likeness!

This is how God's glory is promoted—and you are a most important part of that! Spend time today praising God for His faithfulness, and ask Him to continue His good work in you. It was for this that you were put on earth!

Heavenly Father, I seek to obey You in every way,
so that You can work in me.

CHAPTER TWELVE
Lamed (verses 89-96)

PSALM 119
LAMED
Ox Goad
MEDITATIONS

Lamed, Ox Goad
(pronounced "lah-med")

Lamed is the Hebrew word for "ox goad," a tool used to motivate oxen to go in the right direction. The ox goad was eight feet long. One end was blunt, and was used to dislodge soil from the plow share. The other end had a sharp point. That's the end used to communicate with the ox.

To some extent we can communicate with animals through words, but sometimes a physical message is needed. When an ox was jabbed by the ox goad for the first time, his master gained his attention. After a few encounters with the pointed goad, the ox would begin to react to it. Eventually, the ox could be maneuvered by just the sight of the goad.

The goad represents the Word of God. It is a teacher. It gets our attention, and inspires us to go in the direction our master has intended for us. It causes us to pay attention to His will.

Psalm 119
Verses 89-96

89 *Your word, O LORD, is eternal;*
it stands firm in the heavens.
90 *Your faithfulness continues*
through all generations;
you established the earth, and it endures.
91 *Your laws endure to this day,*
for all things serve you.
92 *If your law had not been my delight,*
I would have perished in my affliction.
93 *I will never forget your precepts,*
for by them you have preserved my life.
94 *Save me, for I am yours;*
I have sought out your precepts.
95 *The wicked are waiting to destroy me,*
but I will ponder your statutes.
96 *To all perfection I see a limit;*
but your commands are boundless.

Sharp Pains from the Word

The Psalmist's Heart: The Eternal Word

In these verses, the psalmist declares the strength of his soul in his days of darkness. The Word of the Lord is settled, and it continues through all generations. His faith triumphs over circumstances.

After tossing about on a sea of troubles, the psalmist leaps confidently to the shore and stands on a rock. God's Word is not uncertain; it is not fickle. It is determined, fixed, sure, and immovable. It is settled in heaven and nothing can reach it there. It cannot be destroyed. It cannot fail.

Your Walk in the Word: The Glint in God's Eye

In Psalm 32: 8,9, we see two kinds of people. Verse eight speaks of an obedient spirit. Once properly instructed and counseled, the master only needs to watch over this person; no further action is required. *"I will instruct you and teach you in the way you should go; I will counsel you and watch over you."*

In verse nine, we see a spirit which needs stronger discipline and constant goading. *"Do not be like the horse or the mule, which have no understanding but must be controlled by bit and bridle or they will not come to you."*

Which are you? *"The words of the wise are like goads, their collected sayings like firmly embedded nails—given by one Shepherd"* (Ecclesiastes 12:11). Do you have to experience the pierce of the goad before you listen to God's law; or can God sit back and allow you "free rein," knowing you will act as He has instructed you?

Your Walk in the World: Struggling Against the Goad

Everyone must experience God's goad sometimes. Saul experienced it on the road to Damascus. He had been persecuting believers, but a battle was going on inside him. Finally, God literally knocked him down.

"Then he fell to the ground, and heard a voice saying to him, 'Saul, Saul, why are you persecuting Me?' And he said, 'Who are You, Lord?' And the Lord said, 'I am Jesus, whom you are persecuting. It is hard for you to kick against the goads' " (Acts 9:4-5 NKJ).

It was impossible for Saul to kick against the goad of God's law, prophets, and writings. God's Word in the hand of Jesus Christ penetrates to the very heart of all human problems. It stirs your will to serve God wholeheartedly. *Lamed* is the Word of God, the most capable goad or motivator of all. Jesus used it on earth and still uses it. Let God's Word goad you today.

His Gift for You: A Loving Prod

Is God goading you? Do you realize in which direction God wants you to go, but still resist His instruction? Yield your heart in obedience to His correction, and you'll be traveling on the righteous path.

Dear Lord,
Be my teacher and give me a heart ready to learn. I will strive to be directed by just a blink of Your eyes, but if it takes a sharp poke to keep me on the right path, then I welcome it. Make me obedient, and keep me traveling in Your direction. Thank You for Your goad of love.

Amen

DEVOTIONS

PSALM 119

LAMED
Ox Goad

MEDITATIONS

Day 89

The Sharp Goad of Faith in the Promise

89   Your word, O LORD, is eternal; it stands firm in the heavens.

The Word stands steadfast in heaven, but it is also faithful on the earth. Job had great opportunity to demonstrate how settled that Word was. He had suffered the loss of everything that he held dear on the earth, yet he was still able to say, *"I know that my Redeemer lives, and that in the end he will stand upon the earth. And after my skin has been destroyed, yet in my flesh I will see God"* (Job 19:25,26).

We talk about the "patience of Job," but even after Job's patience failed, he still held on to his faith. Job said that even if God killed him, he would still trust his Savior.

How does your faith measure up? The righteous live by faith rather than by other graces, because when all else is gone, faith will remain. Faith remains because the promise remains.

Lord, strengthen my faith in Your eternal promises.

Day 90

The Sharp Goad of God's Compass

*90   Your faithfulness continues through all generations;
you established the earth, and it endures.*

God isn't like us. When we create something, we cannot maintain it. All the works of man will eventually crumble and be destroyed. Men make ships, but they can't prevent shipwrecks. Men build houses, but the houses can burn down or decay.

God has not only creative power, but preserving power. He upholds His creation. He confirms in us that He will not cast us off or allow us to perish. He protects and preserves the work of His hands. In the outer region of heaven, we see the sun and moon and all of the heavenly bodies moving in a fixed course where God has set them. God is a constant in the heavens, and in our hearts, as well.

When you feel empty and abandoned, cling to the knowledge that God was there for you before you were born, and that He will preserve you for all eternity.

Father, I thank You for creating me, and for preserving
my life under Your protection.

Day 91

The Sharp Goad of Eternal Law

91 *Your laws endure to this day, for all things serve you.*

In heaven, God has a fixed residence. Our savior, after dying for our sins, sat down at the right of the majesty to see His promises accomplished. By His Word, He will subdue the whole world. All creation serves Him.

God is not affected by the passage of time. Throughout the ages, He has remained exactly the same. If His Word can establish the world and preserve it, then surely it can establish our individual behavior.

Do you prefer to buy your insurance from a company that has been in business for 100 years, or from a new one that opened yesterday? Will you behave according to your own laws, invented by you in your lifetime, or will you live by the Law which has ruled the world since creation? It's an easy choice!

Dear God, align my path with the righteous course
which You set for me.

Day 92

The Sharp Goad of the Mind of God

92 *If your law had not been my delight,*
I would have perished in my affliction.

Think of all the people in the Bible who owed their lives to their delight in God's Law:

- Jonah in the belly of the fish

- Jacob when he had to meet Esau
- the Hebrew children in the fiery furnace
- Daniel in the lion's den
- David facing the giant

God does not forsake you in times of trouble. As long as you hold on to His Word, and keep it as your delight, you will not perish in your affliction.

Without the Word, men may drown themselves in alcohol, commit suicide, or become atheists because they have given up hope. Human philosophy cannot explain suffering nor can it offer comfort. Only the empathy of Jesus, the "man of sorrows," can completely lift us out of emotional depths.

Father, I delight in Your Word, the expression of
Your thoughts, set down just for me.

Day 93

The Sharp Goad of the Golden Pen

93 I will never forget your precepts,
for by them you have preserved my life.

Educators claim we learn best through experience. If a particular scripture speaks to you in a moment of crisis, or if it changes your life or your outlook, you will never forget it. On the other hand, memorizing a speech or poem with no relation to your life can become laborious, or even impossible, despite constant reading and repetition.

Experience teaches, and teaches effectively. When the precept is written on your heart with the golden pen of experience, it is also graven on your memory with a divine pen of grace. That which quickens the heart is sure to quicken the memory.

When the Lord said, "Lazarus, come forth!" he called to Lazarus as if he were alive. The Lord quickened Lazarus by speaking His Word. Don't just read the Word as history, to inform you, but let it inflame you.

Dear Lord, as I read Your Word may it inflame my heart.

Day 94

The Sharp Goad of Service

⁹⁴ *Save me, for I am yours; I have sought out your precepts.*

A good servant diligently searches for that which will make his master happy. Because the psalmist is a servant of God, he eagerly seeks God's will.

A good servant also has a right to expect to be treated well by his master. The psalmist calls out to his Master, "Save me!" That is a wonderful prayer because, in just two words, it expresses the psalmist's faith in God as a savior.

Examine your own heart. Are you a good servant? Do you eagerly search God's Word to find out what He expects of you? If you seek the Lord, you can be sure that He is seeking you. It delights Him when you seek Him with all your heart. To such servants, He guarantees forgiveness, salvation, and eternal life.

Lord, I earnestly seek to know Your desires,
for I want to be Your servant.

Day 95

The Sharp Goad of Wickedness

⁹⁵ *The wicked are waiting to destroy me,*
but I will ponder your statutes.

Wicked men are patient in carrying out their evil plans, but the righteous are patient in meditating upon the ways of God.

The wicked have always hated the righteous: Cain hated Abel; Joseph's brothers all hated him; Saul hated David. Even today, Christians are persecuted all over the world, simply because they choose to follow Jesus.

Be thankful that you are among the hated, and not among the haters. When confronted with such enmity, be watchful over your words and actions. Love your enemies, pray for them, and do good to them at every opportunity. Meditate on the mercy that Jesus exhibited to His enemies, and resolve to be more like Christ.

Father, help me to love my enemies as You have commanded.

Day 96

The Sharp Goad of Perfection

[96] *To all perfection I see a limit; but your commands are boundless.*

Earthly perfection has limits. You may strive to be a perfect housekeeper, yet there will always be another "dust bunny"! Perfectionist accountants still occasionally make computation errors. God's commands are the only perfect thing on earth. God's Word touches every act, word, and thought, and is of such a perfect nature that it can judge the motives and desires of the soul.

Goliath was supposed to be the strongest warrior of the Philistines, but he was overcome (I Samuel 17:4-51). Asahel overtook Abner but Asahel was killed by Abner (II Samuel 2:18-23). Ahithophel was the wisest, but he was fooled (II Samuel 15:31).

Only God's commands are perfect, boundless, and unchangeable. They are higher than heaven. They reach the innermost recesses of the soul, piercing to your most private thoughts.

The Bible tells us that the way of salvation is a narrow way, but to the godly man, it is the most limitless way in the world.

Heavenly Father, Your Word is limitless!

CHAPTER THIRTEEN
Mem (verses 97-104)

PSALM 119
MEM
Water or
Fountain
MEDITATIONS

Mem, Water or Fountain
(pronounced "mem")

The Hebrew word for water is always plural: *waters*. Actually, there are two kinds of water in the Hebrew language: one for the accessible "lower waters" which include rivers, lakes and seas; the other for the upper, inaccessible waters.

When the word *mem* is written in Hebrew, the first "M" is open (like the letter on this page) while the second "M" will be closed. Hebrew scholars say that the first "M" represents the accessible waters, and the second, closed "M" stands for the mysterious waters, unknown and inaccessible.

Water serves many purposes in the Bible. It destroys, as it did in Noah's flood, or it refreshes, like the "still waters" of the 23rd Psalm. It is necessary for life, but can also destroy life. Almost three-quarters of the earth's surface is water, and more than 80 percent of the human body consists of water. Water is at the core of God's creation.

Psalm 119
Verses 97-104

97   *Oh, how I love your law!*
I meditate on it all day long.
98   *Your commands make me*
wiser than my enemies,
for they are ever with me.
99   *I have more insight than all my teachers,*
for I meditate on your statutes.
100   *I have more understanding than the elders,*
for I obey your precepts.
101   *I have kept my feet from every evil path*
so that I might obey your word.
102   *I have not departed from your laws,*
for you yourself have taught me.
103   *How sweet are your words to my taste,*
sweeter than honey to my mouth!
104   *I gain understanding from your precepts;*
therefore I hate every wrong path.

Keys to Success

The Psalmist's Heart: Hoshanna Rabah

This octave contains nothing but praise for the Word of God. There are no requests or petitions. This is not a song of thanksgiving, or a plea for pity, or a cry for deliverance. It is purely and simply a song of delight—a pure and beautiful *Hoshanna Rabah*—"a great Hosanna!"

The theme of water runs throughout the Hebrew Bible. Water can be:
• raging and tumultuous (Psalm 124:5; Isaiah 17:12; Luke 8:24)
• a tool of judgment (Genesis 6:17)
• waters of affliction (Isaiah 30:20)
• purifying (Leviticus 15:13; Numbers 8:7; Ephesians 5:26)
• life-giving (Jeremiah 2:13; Zechariah 14:8; John 4:10; Revelation 7:17)
• a blessing (Isaiah 44:3)

Your Walk in the Word: Come and Drink

The last day of the major Jewish holiday Succot (Feast of Tabernacles) is called "Hoshanna Rabah" or "The Great Hosanna." On that day, priests pray for water for the spring crops, and then pour a pitcher of water onto the ground to acknowledge answered prayer.

It was on Hoshanna Rabah that Jesus made this pronouncement at the temple: "*If anyone is thirsty, let him come to me and drink. Whoever believes in me, as the Scripture has said, streams of living water will flow from within him*'" (John 7:37,38).

Your Walk in the World: Cleansing Fountain

The Israelites had several "cleansing" rituals in which they washed themselves in order to prepare for worshipping God. They washed their hands before they rose from bed, and washed their hands above the wrists before eating. Ceremonial cleansings took place after delivering new babies and after burying the dead.

Do you ever feel "soiled" by the world with its bad messages and devilish philosophies? Before you open your Bible, take a moment to wash your mind and heart clean of the filth of the world, and prepare yourself for the fountain of living water that is about to flow over you!

His Gift for You: No More Thirst

Open your hands and heart to receive the living waters of Jesus! Drink of His love, and you will thirst no more.

Dear Lord,
Your blessings shower down upon me like a refreshing rainfall onto thirsty plants. Thank You for the fountain of wisdom that You prepared for me in the Bible. Help me to taste every life-giving drop. What a wonderful God You are!

Amen

DEVOTIONS

Day 97

The Key to Reverence

⁹⁷ *Oh, how I love your law! I meditate on it all day long.*

The psalmist loves the Word so much that he can't contain himself. Do you obey the Law out of reverence or out of love? Do you love the Law even when it chastises your disobedience?

We love the Law because it is God's. We love the Law for its holiness. It makes us want to be holy. We love it for its wisdom, and we study it to become wise. We love it for its perfection, because we long to be perfect.

This love is not just part-time—it is constant. The more you love the Word, the more you will meditate upon it. The more you meditate upon it, the more you will love it. What a lovely, sacred circle!

Lord, I love Your Law, and long to immerse myself
in its holiness, wisdom, and perfection.

Day 98

The Key of Obedience

⁹⁸ *Your commands make me wiser than my enemies,*
for they are ever with me.

The psalmist celebrates the fact that he is wiser than his enemies because he has studied God's Word. The wisdom of his enemies is earthly, selfish, and comes from the enemy. The wisdom that comes from the Word of God is righteous, just, and true.

Your obedience to God automatically makes you wiser than ungodly men. *"The fear of the LORD is the beginning of wisdom, and knowledge of the Holy One is understanding"* (Proverbs 9:10).

Most school teachers agree that an unruly class is difficult or impossible to teach. Similarly, God can only instruct the obedient. You must humble yourself before Him, acknowledging that you have no wisdom of your own. Open your Bible; He'll give you true understanding.

Father, as I begin my Bible reading each day,
give me a humble and obedient heart.

Day 99

The Key of Insight

⁹⁹ *I have more insight than all my teachers,*
for I meditate on your statutes.

Gaining knowledge consists of learning the facts. Gaining wisdom is understanding and using those facts. Wisdom is knowledge put into daily use.

Is it possible to have a lot of knowledge of Scripture and still not be wise? Yes, it is, if you read and learn just the letter of the Law. It takes the Holy Spirit to impress that Law on your heart and give you understanding. It is the Holy Spirit Who will show you how to put that knowledge to work.

Jesus, as a student, had more insight than all of His teachers. Experience is useful, but the Word is better than experience. Experience takes a long time and the results are never certain. The Word is more exact; it is safer, and it doesn't take long to bear fruit.

It is good to learn from teachers and from elders, but it is best to learn by sitting at the feet of Jesus. Make the Word your constant companion, and Jesus your teacher.

Dear God, fill me with the spirit of insight and
understanding as I read Your Word.

Day 100

The Key to Your Own Heart

¹⁰⁰ *I have more understanding than the elders,*
for I obey your precepts.

In the last two verses, we saw that the psalmist was wiser than his enemies and teachers. Now, we realize he is wiser than the elders. The enemies excel in policy; the teachers in doctrine; the elders in counsel.

Malice sharpens the wit of the psalmist's enemies, and teaches them opposition. Knowledge makes up the learning of teachers, and elders grow wise through long experience. Yet the psalmist is wiser than all of these, for he gains his wisdom by meditating on the Word of God.

When you meditate upon the Word of God, you begin to understand the heart of God. When you begin to understand the heart of God, then you also begin to understand your own heart. Enemies, teachers, and elders cannot give you this understanding.

Father, You know my own heart better than I
do myself. I long to learn from You.

Day 101

The Key to Future Hope

[101] *I have kept my feet from every evil path*
so that I might obey your word.

The psalmist hates sin as much as he loves the Word. Sin strikes at the holiness of God, the glory of God, the nature of God, the being of God, and the Law of God. Anyone who loves God must hate such a weapon against Him.

If you love the Lord, you hate evil. A heart that stores up the Word cannot tolerate sin. *"Know also that wisdom is sweet to your soul; if you find it, there is a future hope for you, and your hope will not be cut off"* (Proverbs 24:14).

Take a loving heart to God, and He will fill it with His Word. *"'This is the covenant I will make with the house of Israel after that time,' declares the LORD. 'I will put my law in their minds and write it on their hearts. I will be their God, and they will be my people'"* (Jeremiah 31:33).

Dear Lord, put Your Law in my
mind and write it on my heart.

Day 102

The Key to Staying on the Path

¹⁰² I have not departed from your laws,
for you yourself have taught me.

The psalmist does not depart from God's laws. There is no room for trial and error here. When we begin to depart just a little, we never know where we will end up.

Did you ever tell a "little white lie"? Have you ever received too much change from a cashier and just put it in your pocket? All by themselves, these little breaches don't seem like much. We tell ourselves that they don't really hurt anybody.

The truth is that the one who is hurt by any little disobedience is you. God has shown you the right way to go. When you start down any path but His, you are flirting with the devil. Let God teach you real obedience.

Lord, teach me to obey You in everything I do and say.

Day 103

The Key to Sweetness

¹⁰³ How sweet are your words to my taste,
sweeter than honey to my mouth!

It is good to keep the Word in your heart, but it is also good to feed on the Word—to taste its sweetness.

It's good to confess the Word. It is sweet to our minds when we think of it, and it will be sweet to our mouths when we speak of it.

If you are hungry, the Word has meat to satisfy you. If you are thirsty, it refreshes you. If you are sick, it heals you. If you are weak, it is a staff to lean on. If the enemy assaults you, it becomes a mighty sword. If you are in darkness, it is a light to your feet. If you are doubtful about which direction to take, it will be a star to lead you. If you are in trouble with God, it will reconcile you. It is the Word of life. Love it, read it, taste it!

Father, I want to receive the engrafted Word.
I want to read it, speak it, taste it.

Day 104

The Key to Success

¹⁰⁴ *I gain understanding from your precepts;*
therefore I hate every wrong path.

This whole section of Psalm 119, verses 97-104, demonstrates a great advance of character on the part of the psalmist. He is growing stronger, bolder, and happier, more able to discern between the precious and the vile.

Are you growing stronger, bolder, and happier day by day? The secret to this growth is love for the Word. Love is the ruler which determines where we spend our time, what we think about, what we talk about, and what we do.

God gave you the Word so that your time, thoughts, words, and actions would bring you prosperity and success: *"Do not let this Book of the Law depart from your mouth; meditate on it day and night, so that you may be careful to do everything written in it. Then you will be prosperous and successful"* (Joshua 1:8).

Heavenly Father, do not let Your Word depart
from my mouth, mind, or heart.

CHAPTER FOURTEEN
Nun (verses 105-112)

PSALM 119
NUN
the Fish
MEDITATIONS

Nun, the Fish
(pronounced "noon")

The letter *nun* represents a fish. Fish is a nourishing food, and fishing has always been an important activity in the Middle East. Scholars attribute the quality of productivity to *nun*. Since fish multiply prolifically, the letter also denotes reproduction or continuance in perpetuity.

The most dramatic reference to fish in the Word is the story of Jonah. His rescue from the belly of a huge fish and his subsequent preaching to the city of Nineveh became a sign for all generations. Jesus Himself referred to Jonah when the skeptics asked Him for a sign (Matthew 12:39-41).

It's not surprising that the early Christians recognized each other by the sign of the fish (the cross did not become the symbol of the Christian Church until several generations later). *Ichthus*, the Greek word for fish, is an acronym for "Jesus, Messiah, God's Son, Savior."

Psalm 119
Verses 105-112

¹⁰⁵ Your word is a lamp to my feet
and a light for my path.
¹⁰⁶ I have taken an oath and confirmed it,
that I will follow your righteous laws.
¹⁰⁷ I have suffered much; preserve
my life, O LORD,
according to your word.
¹⁰⁸ Accept, O LORD, the willing
praise of my mouth,
and teach me your laws.
¹⁰⁹ Though I constantly take my life in my hands,
I will not forget your law.
¹¹⁰ The wicked have set a snare for me,
but I have not strayed from your precepts.
¹¹¹ Your statutes are my heritage forever;
they are the joy of my heart.
¹¹² My heart is set on keeping your decrees
to the very end.

Lights in the Darkness

The Psalmist's Heart: Nourishment from God

All sorts of fish winter in the Atlantic ocean along the coast of Africa. When spring comes, they swim north, and many turn east, traveling through the Straits of Gibraltar and on into the Mediterranean ocean. They follow the currents, reaching the coast of Israel at their plumpest and tastiest, where fishermen catch many species of fish in great abundance. Israel was truly designed by God to provide plenty and prosperity for His people!

The psalmist expresses appreciation for these material gifts, but returns again and again, like a child at Christmas, to his favorite gift: the Word. As nourishing as fish are to the body, the Word is even more nourishing to the soul.

Your Walk in the Word: A Holy Parallel

The parallels between the story of Jonah and the life of Jesus are amazing. The fish that swallowed Jonah was "a gaping void" devouring everything in its path. The world that crucified Jesus was a great emptiness which could not tolerate His truth and righteousness. Jonah was in the belly of the fish for three days, and God rescued him from what appeared to be sure death. God raised Jesus up from the grave after three days. Jonah's greatest service to God came after his rescue. Jesus' greatest effect on the world came after His Resurrection.

Your Walk in the World: Proof Positive

Ungodly men to this day try to explain away the Resurrection of Jesus Christ. Has anyone ever told you that "Jesus was a great teacher, but He wasn't God"? Isn't it amazing how the devil can work against acceptance of events that were witnessed by hundreds of people?

Why would the devil spend so much energy convincing people that the Resurrection never happened? Because the Resurrection is the sure sign that God accepted and approved the work of Jesus. It is proof of all that Jesus told us and proof that He now sits on the right hand of God.

When doubts nag at you (and they will—Satan is tireless!), remember the Resurrection. Hundreds saw Jesus die, and hundreds saw Him alive afterward. The Resurrection is the undeniable proof that Jesus was the One sent from God to save you. Praise Him!

His Gift for You: A Bountiful Feast

God created the Promised Land for His people, with plenty of nourishment for the body. In the same way, God prepared the Holy Bible to nourish you. Take up His gift, and feed your heart, soul, and mind.

Father,
Thank You that You have provided for my every need. You have given me so many gifts, but my favorite gift is the bountiful feast of Your Word. In the Bible, You have given me everything I need to nourish my soul, to know You, and to become more and more like You each day. Help me to taste, chew, and digest this feast!

Amen

DEVOTIONS

PSALM 119

NUN
the Fish

MEDITATIONS

Day 105

Light Up a Dark World

105 Your word is a lamp to my feet and a light for my path.

As visitors to this world, we are often called to walk in its darkness. Without the light-giving Word, we would slip and fall.

The Word is to be used personally, practically, and habitually to light your way and let you see what lies in the path that He has laid out.

When darkness settles down all around you, the Word of the Lord is a flaming torch; it reveals the path. Jesus is a light for your path, a lamp by night, a light by day, and a delight at all times.

"The sun will no more be your light by day, nor will the brightness of the moon shine on you, for the LORD will be your everlasting light, and your God will be your glory" (Isaiah 60:19).

Take the Word into your heart and it becomes a lamp within your soul. It will light your way forever.

Lord, I sing the praises of the light which
shines in the darkness of the world.

Day 106

Light Up Your Promises

106 I have taken an oath and confirmed it,
that I will follow your righteous laws.

Have you ever made a promise to God or in God's name? Wedding vows and oaths taken in court are examples of vows to God, but promises to God can also be made in private—just between you and God. It is important for righteous people to keep their promises, but it is essential to keep promises made to God.

Making a religious vow is serious business. It can be a very good thing, because your conscience will be pricked to keep the vow. On the other hand, a vow unfulfilled is a major moral breach.

Our ability to keep the promises we make to God is dependent on the movement of the Spirit. Drink in the Word, and ask the Spirit to dwell within you. With His strength, you can keep all your promises.

Father, with Your help, I will fulfill the promise
I have made to follow You.

Day 107

Light Up Your Joy

¹⁰⁷ *I have suffered much; preserve my life,*
O LORD, according to your word.

We live in an imperfect world, so we are bound to suffer. Fortunately, God has foreseen our suffering, and set in place a plan that preserves us.

"No temptation has seized you except what is common to man. And God is faithful; he will not let you be tempted beyond what you can bear. But when you are tempted, he will also provide a way out so that you can stand up under it" (I Corinthians 10:13).

God will not let you suffer hardships greater than your ability to bear them. He will protect you from temptation, too—always providing a way for you to avoid falling into the enemy's trap.

With such a loving God protecting you, surely you can rejoice! *"...be content with what you have, because God has said, 'Never will I leave you; never will I forsake you'"* (Hebrews 13:5).

Dear God, I rejoice that You will never forsake me!

Day 108

Light Up Your Offerings

108   Accept, O LORD, the willing praise of my mouth,
and teach me your laws.

The praise from the psalmist's mouth is "willing praise"—a freewill offering to the Lord. The Lord loves freewill offerings. They are mentioned 14 times in the Old Testament!

" *I will sacrifice a freewill offering to you; I will praise your name, O LORD, for it is good*" (Psalm 54:6).

People who love the Lord, love giving back to Him. The gifts may be material, and those are important, but God loves the offerings of praise that come from your mouth. The light has to shine not just in your heart, but it must shine from your words, as well.

Father, my heart is so full of love for You that
I just have to shout Your praises!

Day 109

Light Up Your Life

109   Though I constantly take my life in my hands,
I will not forget your law.

A life without light cannot be blessed. In the world, we enjoy the sun by day, and the moon by night, but our spirits crave the light provided by God's Word.

Life is very fragile. Paul declared that he died daily (I Corinthians 15:31). We are only safe in the hand of God. Security can only be found on the path that is revealed by the light of the Word.

Christ Himself is a lamp and a light. He was a light to Peter when the angel stood by him in the prison and the light shined about him (Acts 12:7). He was a light to Paul when the light from heaven shined round about him (Acts 9:3). God will be a light to you, too. You only have to ask.

Dear Lord, light my path; be a lamp unto my feet.

Day 110

Light Up the Snares of the Wicked

110 The wicked have set a snare for me,
but I have not strayed from your precepts.

The world is full of snares set by the enemy. Many times the enemy is disguised as a well-intentioned friend. Here are some of the common snares you must guard against.

- Theological snares set by intellectuals who study the Word but are not indwelt by the Spirit
- False accusations by jealous people
- False flattery by deceitful people
- False charity, by people who like to brag about their generosity, yet whose hearts do not belong to God

How can you protect yourself from these snares? Obedience to God is the only sure path to safety. God keeps those who keep His Word.

Dear Lord, cast a light on the snares of the world,
and keep me safe from them.

Day 111

Light Up Your Heart

111 Your statutes are my heritage forever;
they are the joy of my heart.

Statutes can refer to testimonies. Scripture contains testimonies regarding God Himself. Scripture testifies of His wisdom, His power, His justice, His goodness, and His truth.

Each book is a distinct testimony. The book of Genesis is a testimony of His creative power, His justice in drowning the world, and His goodness in saving Noah. The book of Exodus provides a testimony of His providence in bringing the people out of Egypt, and His wisdom in giving them the Law.

In the New Testament, the statutes are of Jesus and His humility, His humanness, His power in working miracles, His wisdom in answering the Pharisees, and His patience and love through the torment He suffered.

The Bible is our inheritance, for this life and for all eternity.

Father, I am so glad You adopted me to be an heir
to your precious statutes.

Day 112

Light Up Your Target

*112   My heart is set on keeping your
decrees to the very end.*

Did you know that guided missiles actually travel in very crooked paths? They are set toward a certain objective, but wind currents constantly throw them off their aim. That's when their carefully programmed computers work to bring them back on target.

Will the psalmist perfectly obey God all of his life? This may be his plan, but, being only human, he will stray from time to time. In what direction is your heart pointed? Even if your heart's compass is set toward God, you may find yourself going off course now and then. Be sure that your heart's computer is properly programmed—with the Word of God—so that you will quickly be put back on target.

With the proper programming, you will consistently follow the path that God set out for you, and you will, in the end, hit your target.

*Heavenly Father, I direct my heart
toward You. Keep me on course.*

CHAPTER FIFTEEN
Samech (verses 113-120)

Samech, Prop or Staff
(pronounced "sah-mekh")

Jewish scholars describe *samech* as protection. It has an active side (God's protection of us) and a passive side (our reliance on God for His support and protection). Another aspect of *samech* is the concept of memory. It is our memory of the Word of God that gives us the faith to rely on Him, that supports or props us up in time of human weakness.

In the Old Testament, God frequently used the staff as an earthly sign of His power. Moses took his staff when he pleaded with Pharaoh (Exodus 4:17). The Israelites were ready with their staffs in their hands on the night they left Egypt (Exodus 12:11). The Red Sea parted when Moses raised his staff over it (Exodus 14:16).

Godly men often took up the staff in times of trouble. It represented God's presence and protection. David took his staff with him when he went to face Goliath (I Samuel 17:40). Jacob took his staff when he went out to find a wife (Genesis 32:10).

Godless countries were often referred to as having a broken staff (II Kings 18:21, Jeremiah 48:17).

Psalm 119
Verses 113-120

113   *I hate double-minded men,*
but I love your law.
114   *You are my refuge and my shield;*
I have put my hope in your word.
115   *Away from me, you evildoers,*
that I may keep the commands of my God!
116   *Sustain me according to your promise,*
and I will live;
do not let my hopes be dashed.
117   *Uphold me, and I will be delivered;*
I will always have regard for your decrees.
118   *You reject all who stray from your decrees,*
for their deceitfulness is in vain.
119   *All the wicked of the earth you*
discard like dross;
therefore I love your statutes.
120   *My flesh trembles in fear of you;*
I stand in awe of your laws.

The Lift That Doesn't Let You Down

The Psalmist's Heart: Eternal Protection

Throughout Psalm 119, the psalmist repeatedly stresses his total and complete dependence on God. He trusts in God's protection even when there is no earthly hope. With dependence on the staff of God's presence, there is nothing to fear:

"Even though I walk through the valley of the shadow of death, I will fear no evil, for you are with me; your rod and your staff, they comfort me" (Psalm 23:4).

God is the staff of His people. We strive to remember Him at all times. We can live in the peaceful knowledge that His protection is mighty and eternal.

Your Walk in the Word: Jesus is Your Staff

Throughout the Old Testament, the physical staff is the medium for miracles, and the sign of God's presence. In the New Testament, Jesus becomes that staff. He is God's presence on earth, and He is the source of all our comfort and security.

It is interesting that when Jesus sent the disciples out to teach, *"He told them: 'Take nothing for the journey—no staff, no bag, no bread, no money, no extra tunic'"* (Luke 9:3). He was telling them that they had no need of the old, traditional sign of God's presence. They had no need of physical provisions. Because they had God's own Son. In Him was God's provision for every one of their needs. Jesus would be their staff! He would prop them up.

Your Walk in the World: The Power of Jesus

When Jesus was arrested, the soldiers mocked Him. We all remember the crown of thorns which they wove for Him, but did you realize that they mocked Him with a staff, as well? *"...They put a staff in his right hand and knelt in front of him and mocked him. 'Hail, king of the Jews!' they said"* (Matthew 27:29).

The soldiers didn't want to believe that Jesus was really a king. He did not wear the purple robes of royalty, live in luxurious palace, or lead a powerful army. How could this simple peasant be a king?

Today, ungodly people still look to the material world for signs of power. They admire those who are rich, talented, or famous. Godly people know that the real power—the only power that counts—is the power of Jesus' love.

His Gift for You:

God has given you the most reliable prop of all: Jesus' love! It is a staff that you can count on for support in the world.

Dear God,
Thank You for providing a strong staff of support and protection in the love and sacrifice of Your holy Son. Help me to remember, even when the world presents obstacles, that Your sturdy staff will hold me up, and keep me from stumbling.

Amen

DEVOTIONS

Day 113

His Law Lifts You Up

> [113] *I hate double-minded men, but I love your law.*

Godly people, like the psalmist, hate the double-minded: people who say one thing and do another. Such wickedness always leads to confusion and worry. People who lie have to strain and struggle to keep their lies straight.

How much more peaceful it is to live a life with a single purpose: the way of God. When you live in truth, you never have to worry about keeping your stories straight! The thoughts of men are vanity, but the thoughts of God are verity.

When you love the Law, it becomes a law of love. You will find that the Lord is your hiding place. It is a happy place to be. Cling to Him with all your heart!

> *Lord, I cling to Your truth and Your love.*

Day 114

His Arms Lift You Up

> [114] *You are my refuge and my shield;*
> *I have put my hope in your word.*

The psalmist wants to keep the Law, but he needs the Lord of the Law to keep him. He takes God as his hiding place.

Aren't you delighted that you, too, can take God as your hiding place? Your hiding place is not made of paper, reeds, or rotten timber. It is a place of strength, because your hiding place is Jesus! He is the Rock of ages, the mighty God, sitting in a high place.

When you need to hide from the wickedness and lies of the world, rejoice that your hiding place is the Rock set in a high place—as high as heaven! Jesus is Jacob's ladder that connects you to heaven.

Your hiding place is too high for man or devils to reach. Rest peacefully, for no creature can scale those high and mighty walls. Jesus is hiding You in His Holy arms.

Father, I rest peacefully within the security of Your Son.

Day 115

His Commands Lift You Up

115 *Away from me, you evildoers,*
that I may keep the commands of my God!

The psalmist knew an important fact: you cannot walk with one foot in the devil's world and the other in God's world. If you are married to God's commandments, you will not commit adultery with the lies of the world.

David purged his palace of parasites: people who did not know God. He refused to harbor them under his roof. It can be very hard to resist the parasites of the world, especially when they seem to be having so much fun! Just remember that the devil packages sin in attractive wrappings. Don't be deceived!

You are called to love everyone, but you are not called to spend time with everyone. Pray for your lost friends, but don't hang around them when they are doing evil. Choose eternal joy over temporary fun. Immerse yourself in the life-giving Word, which ascends far above the evil of the world.

Dear God, keep me away from evildoers,
for I am married to Your commands.

Day 116

His Hope Lifts You Up

116 *Sustain me according to your promise, and I will live;*
do not let my hopes be dashed.

It is easy to hope when you've already experienced hope. The more you read the Word, the more hope you will have in God. He always keeps His promises. This is proven over and over again in the Bible. The more you understand about God's history of faithfulness to His people, the more you can trust in His faithfulness to you.

How wonderful hope is! Without it, you cannot be truly happy. You can have all of your circumstances stripped to a bare minimum, but if you have hope for tomorrow, you will survive.

When you go after heavenly pursuits, your soul will be raised up like a soaring kite.

Father, lift up my heart,
for I have hope in Your faithfulness.

Day 117

His Word Lifts You Up

117 *Uphold me, and I will be delivered;*
I will always have regard for your decrees.

For the godly man who loves the Word, the Lord will always be a prop or a support. He will uphold you and deliver you.

How does God hold you up? He upholds all things by the Word of His power. He holds you up with His Holy Spirit. He holds you up with the administration of angels: *"For he will command his angels concerning you to guard you in all your ways; they will lift you up in their hands, so that you will not strike your foot against a stone"* (Psalm 91:11,12).

The psalmist promises that he will always love God's laws—they are the foundation that holds him up and keeps him safe against worldly trials and tribulations.

Dear Lord, thank You for holding me up in
Your wisdom and Your love.

Day 118

His Knowledge Lifts You Up

118 *You reject all who stray from your decrees,*
for their deceitfulness is in vain.

Godly people hate vain thoughts of deceitful men. Vain thoughts are useless and harmful. They include unclean thoughts, prideful thoughts, thoughts of revenge, envy, covetousness, and distrust.

Vanity is always unprofitable; it has no substance or weight, so it floats to the top of life like scum. It is foolish, frail, and inconstant. Vain thoughts are fleeting; they perish like bubbles. Worst of all, they draw your heart away from the worship of God. Turn instead to the weighty, precious Word of the Lord; seek only His knowledge. *"The eyes of the LORD keep watch over knowledge, but he frustrates the words of the unfaithful"* (Proverbs 22:12).

> *Dear Lord, show me any vain thoughts that I might*
> *harbor, and put me back on Your path of truth.*

Day 119

His Righteousness Lifts You Up

> [119] *All the wicked of the earth you discard like dross;*
> *therefore I love your statutes.*

How does God consider the wicked of the earth? They are like dross:

1. Dross obscures the luster and glory of the metal that it covers up. Rust encompasses and hides gold so that neither the nature nor the luster of it can be seen.
2. Dross deceives. The dross of silver is like silver, but it is not silver. The dross of gold is like gold, but it is not gold.
3. Dross is not cleansed by fire. When you put dross into a furnace, it doesn't change.
4. Dross is worthless.
5. Dross is useless, and must be rejected and discarded.
6. Dross is offensive. It eats into the metal and endangers it. The goldsmith must put the metal into the fire to separate it from the dross. That's the way God treats the wicked.

Don't you love the perfect righteousness of your God Who loves you?

> *Father, separate me from the dross, and keep me pure*
> *through the fire of Your Word.*

Day 120

His Faithfulness Lifts You Up

¹²⁰ My flesh trembles in fear of you;
I stand in awe of your laws.

This is such a gorgeous verse! True religion consists of a proper mixture of fear of God and hope in His mercy. Godly people both tremble in fear and stand in awe of His Word.

Turn to the Word and you will discover a wonderful, awesome retreat. It will nourish and sustain you. It is a secret place of faith and spiritual safety. God's faithfulness is your great hope. He won't turn you over to the devil. *"...Jesus Christ, who is the faithful witness, the firstborn from the dead, and the ruler of the kings of the earth. To him who loves us and has freed us from our sins by his blood,..."* (Revelation 1:5).

His faithfulness to you enables your faithfulness to Him. *"This calls for patient endurance on the part of the saints who obey God's commandments and remain faithful to Jesus"* (Revelation 14:12). What a wonderful gift exchange!

Heavenly Father, I tremble when I consider Your great
faithfulness. I strive to be faithful, likewise, to You.

CHAPTER SIXTEEN
Ayin (verses 121-128)

PSALM 119

AYIN
the Eye

MEDITATIONS

Ayin, the Eye
(pronounced "ah-yin")

Ayin, the eye, represents both sight and insight: seeing the outward form as well as the inner being. *"But the LORD said to Samuel, '...The LORD does not look at the things man looks at. Man looks at the outward appearance, but the LORD looks at the heart'"* (I Samuel 16:7).

The tiny opening of the eye is our window on the world. At the same time, the eye is the only window into the soul—the only means we have of discerning a person's true nature. The Lord, however, can see right into the heart. His view is always accurate. *"The eyes of the LORD are everywhere, keeping watch on the wicked and the good"* (Proverbs 15:3).

Just as the eye is the source of tears, *ayin* can also refer to a "fountain or flowing of water." Fourteen cities mentioned in the Bible which begin with *ayin* are all known for having great fountains at their center.

Ayin can also refer to seers or prophets, people whose eyes have been opened by God to see things that most people do not see.

Psalm 119
Verses 121-128

121   *I have done what is righteous and just;*
    do not leave me to my oppressors.
122   *Ensure your servant's well-being;*
    let not the arrogant oppress me.
123   *My eyes fail, looking for your salvation,*
    looking for your righteous promise.
124 *Deal with your servant according to your love*
    and teach me your decrees.
125   *I am your servant; give me discernment*
    that I may understand your statutes.
126   *It is time for you to act, O LORD;*
    your law is being broken.
127   *Because I love your*
    commands more than gold,
    more than pure gold,
128 *and because I consider all your precepts right,*
    I hate every wrong path.

Keep Your Eye on the Goal

The Psalmist's Heart: Clear Vision in Times of Distress

In these eight verses we see a man who is true to God, living in a time when those in power are trying to make void the Word of God. The verses open with a note of depression. The eyes of the psalmist fail to perceive salvation. His distress is expressed in prayer, and the result is a victory for faith.

The psalmist's prayers are a supreme evidence of faith. He asks for mercy, teaching, and understanding. Everything ends with a declaration of certainty that the precepts of Jehovah are right.

Your Walk in the Word: Fountains of Tears

Jesus saw things that were not visible to the human eye: *"...I saw Satan fall like lightning from heaven"* (Luke 10:18). When Jesus first saw Nathaniel, He told Nathaniel that He had seen him sitting under a fig tree.

Jesus wept a lot. Those with the ability to see this world clearly tend to weep for it. Jesus wept for Jerusalem; He wept for the dead Lazarus. Jesus was often compared to Jeremiah, the "weeping prophet."

Were all the tears of the prophets, the Messiah, and many martyrs and sufferers in vain? Certainly not! God has recorded and preserved every one of those tears, and He makes them into fountains and pools for the sustenance of His people.

Your Walk in the World: A Light to the Eyes

The world sees things differently than God does. As the old saying goes: "There is more here than meets the eye." From time to time, God helped people in the Bible see more than the physical eye could perceive:

"Then the LORD opened Balaam's eyes, and he saw the angel of the LORD standing in the road with his sword drawn. So he bowed low and fell facedown" (Numbers 22:31).

"And Elisha prayed, 'O LORD, open his eyes so he may see.' Then the LORD opened the servant's eyes, and he looked and saw the hills full of horses and chariots of fire all around Elisha" (II Kings 6:17).

It takes God's touch to open our eyes to the real truth. The world is focused on physical things which can be seen. You go to the optometrist to be given 20-20 vision. God is the optometrist Who gives you 20-20 vision of the heart. *"The precepts of the LORD are right, giving joy to the heart. The commands of the LORD are radiant, giving light to the eyes"* (Psalms 19:8).

His Gift for You: 20-20 Vision of the Heart

Through God's Word, you can achieve clarity about your life and your future. You will see the world as it really is, and you will begin to focus your vision on the kingdom of God.

Dear God,
Open my eyes to Your truth, Your faithfulness, and Your wisdom.
The greatest vision I could have would be to look upon Your face. Let
Your radiance illuminate my heart and my soul, so that the darkness
of the world fades into nothingness. I want to focus on Your beauty,
Your power, and Your love. Fill my eyes with a holy light.

Amen

DEVOTIONS

PSALM 119

AYIN
the Eye

MEDITATIONS

Day 121

Keep Your Eye on the Word

> 121 *I have done what is righteous and just;*
> *do not leave me to my oppressors.*

This verse deals with a test of faith. Suppose that you need a favor from your boss at work. Are you more likely to get that favor if you have been doing your job well? Would you even dare to ask a favor if your work has been sloppy?

When you follow God's directions, you will find more confidence to ask Him for help whenever you need it. Here, the psalmist reminds God of his upright conduct, and then appeals to God for deliverance from oppression.

It is so encouraging to see this psalmist, while under attack from all sides, cling to his faith in God's Word. There are nine thematic words, one of which appears in almost every verse of Psalm 119: law, testimony, precept, statute, commandment, judgment, word, and way. This entire psalm is dedicated to the Word of God, and the great comfort, protection, and deliverance which can be found there.

Lord, starting today, I am going to spend more time in Your
Word, the only sure source of comfort.

Day 122

Keep Your Eye on Jesus

> 122 *Ensure your servant's well-being; let not the arrogant oppress me.*

God is the ultimate insurance policy! Here, the psalmist asks God to be his insurance policy against the oppression of arrogant men. He needs God to stand between him and his enemies.

This was the same request that Hezekiah made in his troubles: *"I cried like a swift or thrush, I moaned like a mourning dove. My eyes grew weak as I looked to the heavens. I am troubled; O Lord, come to my aid!"* (Isaiah 38:14). It is the prayer of Job for a mediator to stand up for him: *"If only there were someone to arbitrate between us, to lay his hand upon us both,..."* (Job 9:33).

This is also the cry of the Church. The Bible says *"He who puts up security for another will surely suffer, but whoever refuses to strike hands in pledge is safe"* (Proverbs 11:15). Jesus became our security, and He suffered for it, too. If there was ever a gap-stander, it is Jesus Christ.

Father, I thank You for sending your Son as a
gap-stander for me, ensuring my eternal life.

Day 123

Keep Your Eye on His Mercy

123 *My eyes fail, looking for your salvation,*
looking for your righteous promise.

This verse describes one of the darkest times for a believer. Sometimes, our eyes fail, looking for His promise. Eyes are tender things, and so are faith, hope, and expectancy. If it has been a long time since you have heard His voice, or experienced His blessings, your faith may begin to fade. This can be painful.

Praise God that even in these dark, dry times, there is hope. God's mercy is there for you, and He knows just what you need. The mercy is that even if our eyes fail, God doesn't. Wait for Him, and He will restore your eyes, your heart, and your faith.

God says He will not give us more than we can bear. Come before Him as His servant, and ask for His mercy. Ask Him to restore your faith. He has promised to grant your request!

Dear God, I know You are there even when I can't see You or hear You.

Day 124

Keep Your Eye on the Master

124 *Deal with your servant according to your love*
and teach me your decrees.

In ancient times, it was the duty of a master to clear the name of an accused slave. The master was responsible for rescuing his slave from those who tried to oppress him. The master would show mercy to his servant, even if he dealt severely with strangers.

This is why the psalmist asks God to deal with him as a servant. We need the love, kindness, and mercy of a benevolent master. God has promised us just such a relationship. The Hebrew word for *love* in this verse really means "the love and kindness of a friend." A good master is really a friend to his servant.

Finally, a good master teaches his slave. He carefully explains and demonstrates just what he expects. In all respects, the Lord is a wonderful Master: our Protector, our Teacher, our Friend.

Father, I am so grateful to be Your servant,
Your student, and Your friend.

Day 125

Keep Your Eye on the Teacher

125 *I am your servant; give me discernment*
that I may understand your statutes.

The psalmist, an educated Hebrew, has prophets, rabbis, and Levites to teach him, but he indicates that all this teaching is nothing unless God speaks to his heart.

For our Ruler to become our Teacher is a great honor which proceeds from God's grace. The psalmist asks God for knowledge, but he also asks Him for understanding and discernment. Usually, the pupil gets information from the teacher, but the student must find the understanding on his own. Here, the psalmist is asking both from God.

Our trouble has always been God's opportunity. When the earth was without form, the Spirit came and moved on the face of the waters. When society is in chaos, won't the Spirit also come if we cry out to Him? God will always stretch out His hand to the faithful, and He will always defend His truth.

Dear Lord, as I read Your Word, give me not just knowledge,
but also understanding.

Day 126

Keep Your Eye on the Victory

126   It is time for you to act, O LORD; your law is being broken.

The last six verses have dealt with the testing of faith and the activity of faith. This verse introduces the victory of faith. There is no doubt that God will take action against those who break His Law. It is just a matter of time. The action requested in these verses is defense of the righteous and punishment for the wicked.

In the last two verses, the psalmist asked for understanding concerning those who were oppressing him. Apparently, the discernment that he received from God was that he should do nothing. God will take the appropriate actions at the appropriate times.

What wonderful wisdom! Judgments against the wicked and defense of the obedient are to be handled by God, not by us. Our job is to pray for our oppressors, and to wait for God's response in His perfect time.

Dear Lord, I turn over to You all thoughts of revenge against my oppressors. I will wait for You to act.

Day 127

Keep Your Eye on Spiritual Gold

127   Because I love your commands more than gold,
more than pure gold,

Saints improve under pressure, and are bettered by even the worst circumstances. Even when the world despises God's Law, holiness is bestowed upon the godly. It is interesting that some eminent saints in the early church were those of Caesar's household (Philippians 4:22). Those who kept God's name lived where Satan's throne was located (Revelation 2:13). Zeal for God often grows hotter through opposition.

God's Word is more precious than gold. We Christians are to be spiritual misers, loving the Word above all, and hiding it in our hearts where the devil cannot reach it.

We don't have to be afraid of covetousness in spiritual things. Rather, we should covet the Word so that it grows richer, and more precious in value. Loving the Word is great progress in godliness.

Father, I love Your Word more than anything I possess.

Day 128

Keep Your Eye on His Precepts

128 and because I consider all your precepts right,
I hate every wrong path.

The natural man hates the commandments of God. They're contrary to his nature. The born-again man hates his own corruption, loves the Word, and wants to be conformed to it. It is a comfort that we love the commandments even when we don't fully obey them.

The righteous man squares all his actions by right rule. Carnal reason doesn't bias him. Corrupt practices don't sway him. The more God's sacred Word directs him, the more he will hate every false way.

A good test of our love for God and His Word is to consider the opposite: do we hate sin and unrighteousness? When we love God with infinite intensity, we will love good with the same intensity.

Heavenly Father, I love Your Word, and strive every day to obey it.
Give me an intense hatred for disobedience to Your commands.

CHAPTER SEVENTEEN
Pe (verses 129-136)

PSALM 119

PE
the Mouth

MEDITATIONS

Pe, the Mouth
(pronounced "pey")

The mouth makes man a human being able to fulfill the ultimate purpose of creation: to sing the praises of the Almighty, and to speak out His Word.

The ability to speak is a joy of human life and sets us apart from animals. Humans were given an ability to speak and communicate, using words. It is one of the essential vehicles of the Creator.

Hebrew scholars recognized the mouth as the source of silence, as well. Speech is important, but sometimes it can be just as important to keep your mouth closed!

Psalm 119
Verses 129-136

129   *Your statutes are wonderful;*
       therefore I obey them.
130   *The unfolding of your words gives light;*
    it gives understanding to the simple.
131   *I open my mouth and pant,*
    longing for your commands.
132   *Turn to me and have mercy on me,*
    as you always do to those
      who love your name.
133 *Direct my footsteps according to your word;*
    let no sin rule over me.
134   *Redeem me from the oppression of men,*
    that I may obey your precepts.
135   *Make your face shine upon your servant*
    and teach me your decrees.
136   *Streams of tears flow from my eyes,*
    for your law is not obeyed.

The Power of the Mouth

The Psalmist's Heart: The Perfect Gift

The speech of man is a wonderful gift of the Creator, but the words that come from God's mouth are life itself. In fact, God created the world just by speaking. Whenever He speaks, His words are perfect, powerful, and unchangeable. His Words can never be reversed or refuted, because His Word is forever established in heaven.

What makes God's Word so different from ours is that His nature is perfectly righteous, so His words are perfect. When God speaks, it is with absolute certainty.

All of Psalm 119 is a song of praise for God's Word. When God gave the Word to man, the psalmist says, it was the ultimate gift—the absolute proof of God's love for us.

Your Walk in the Word: The Words of God's Mouth

When God placed words in a prophet's mouth, the prophet's mouth became like God's mouth. *"Then the LORD reached out his hand and touched my mouth and said to me, 'Now, I have put my words in your mouth' "* (Jeremiah 1:9). The Lord told Moses: *"I will raise up for them a prophet like you from among their brothers; I will put my words in his mouth, and he will tell them everything I command him. If anyone does not listen to my words that the prophet speaks in my name, I myself will call him to account"* (Deuteronomy 18:18,19). This prophet, of course, is Jesus Christ.

How do we know this prophet is Jesus? Jesus was like Moses in many ways. Both were endangered by tyrants who killed male babies. Both were spared death by God-fearing parents. Both miraculously spent their childhoods in safety in Egypt. Both were scorned and misunderstood by their brothers. Both were willing to offer their lives so that Israel would be reconciled to God (Exodus 32:30-34; John 11:49-52; Acts 3:25, 26; II Corinthians 5:18,19).

Whenever Jesus spoke, God spoke through Him. *Pe* represents the mouth and the words of our great Shepherd.

Your Walk in the World: Overflow of the Heart

God designed man's power of speech for good and great purposes. He gave that power to Adam and Eve. Since then, it has often been warped and misused. The mouth can be a wicked weapon, cutting through the heart and causing great pain.

There is a strong connection between the heart and the mouth. *"You brood of vipers, how can you who are evil say anything good? For out of the overflow of the heart the mouth speaks"* (Matthew 12:34). This is why all of Jesus' words were good and true. It wasn't just His words, it was the character of His heart that distinguished Him from all others. *"He committed no sin, and no deceit was found in his mouth. When they hurled their insults at him, he did not retaliate; when he suffered, he made no threats. Instead, he entrusted himself to him who judges justly"* (I Peter 2:22,23).

Jesus' words reflected His perfection, and God's truth. When it came to revenge and retaliation against those who spoke evil, He chose to keep His mouth shut, leaving judgment to His Father.

His Gift for You: The Words of His Mouth

God's Word is all powerful; His voice brought all creation into being. His voice will awaken the dead from all past generations; His words will never pass away. Truly the gift of His Word is the greatest gift that a loving God could bestow on His children.

Dear God,
How precious is Your gift to me—the gift of Your Word. I cherish it because it contains the truth and direction that I need to live a godly life. Each time I open my Bible, I praise Your Holy Name. Help me to use Your gift as You intended: to learn, to grow, and to become more like You day by day.

Amen

DEVOTIONS

Day 129

The Power of Metamorphosis

129 Your statutes are wonderful; therefore I obey them.

The testimonies of the Lord are life changing. No one can be completely obedient to the Word on his own. You cannot ever be a *good* person on your own. It simply is not in your power. The psalmist says that he obeys God's commands *because* they are so wonderful.

Immersing yourself in the Word will bring about miraculous transformation. When your heart is saturated with His truth, you will find yourself becoming more obedient without any special effort on your part. It is the strength and power of the Word, not your own strength and power, which creates an obedient heart in you.

What a wonderful gift! You don't have to work at being "good people." No matter how hard you tried, you would be sure to fail. Instead, turn your heart and life over to God, and *He* will bring about this miraculous metamorphosis.

Lord, transform me through the truth and saving grace of Your Word.

Day 130

The Power of the Face of Christ

130 The unfolding of your words gives light;
it gives understanding to the simple.

From the Word of God, the light of life shines brightly. As we look intently at His Word, that light reveals God's face to us. *"...in your light, we see light"* (Psalm 36:9). *"For God, who said, 'Let light shine out of darkness,' made his light shine in our hearts to give us the light of the knowledge of the glory of God in the face of Christ"* (II Corinthians 4:6).

The greatest experience you can ever have is to see the face of God. In the Old Testament, people had to hide themselves from the face of God. They put on a veil to separate them from the overwhelming glory of that face.

Jesus came to remove that veil. Through Him, we can come face to face with God. Peter, James, and John were the first to have this breathtaking experience at the transfiguration (Matthew 17:2). Today, you, too, can receive this transforming gift: *"And we, who with unveiled faces all reflect the Lord's glory, are being transformed into his likeness with ever-increasing glory, which comes from the Lord, who is the Spirit"* (II Corinthians 3:18).

Father, I long to look upon the precious face of Your Son, Jesus Christ.

Day 131

The Power of Human Longing

131   *I open my mouth and pant, longing for your commands.*

The psalmist has such a deep longing for the Word of God! Each of us is born with this longing—with an emptiness that only the Bible can fill up.

The Bible is the heart and soul of God. It is the library of the Holy Spirit. It contains all the things which we are to believe and all the things which we are to practice. It makes us wise unto salvation. It is the standard of truth and the polestar that directs us to heaven.

Scripture is the compass by which the rudder of our will is to be steered. It is the field in which Christ, the pearl of great price, is hid. It is the rock from which flows the living water.

How do you know Scripture is the Word of God? By the light that shines in it. You won't walk in the darkness if you have the light of life.

Dear God, fill my deep hunger for Your Word,
Your Light, and Your Life.

Day 132

The Power of Love

132   *Turn to me and have mercy on me,*
as you always do to those who love your name.

God showers mercy down on the godly. Anyone who carefully observes the joyful serenity of believers will want to have those same gifts. "How can I get what you have?" they are likely to ask.

How glorious that the answer is so simple. The price of God's mercy is not perfect behavior—of which none of us is capable! The only price is to love Him. Loving Him is such a wonderful and glorious adventure that it hardly seems as if you are paying a price at all!

Once again, God has made it so easy! Because you love Him, you receive His mercy. The more you experience His tender mercies, the more you love Him! Soon your heart and your life are full of only Him— and those around you will want to know where you got all that happiness. Won't it be fun to tell them about God's great love for you and for them?

Father, my love for You is so great that I can scarcely express it.
How I cherish the mercy which you shower down on me.

Day 133

The Power of God's Road Map

133 Direct my footsteps according to your word;
let no sin rule over me.

We are all on a journey in this life. On this journey, we can choose the path to God, or the path of evil. Our fleshly nature wants to walk the devil's path. Left without a direction or plan, our feet will naturally carry us down the wrong path.

It is important to let God direct our steps. The road to heaven or to hell is traveled one step at a time. Every step must be guarded zealously against the attacks of the enemy. Satan loves to put up false road signs to turn you away from God. God gives power over any fleshly inclination that would lead you to believe the road signs of the enemy. Only God can guide your footsteps so that you do not stumble and fall.

Don't trust your own judgment. Instead, put every step you take in God's hands. He alone knows the road which you must follow. He loves you, and wants to see you arrive home safely. Let Him show you the way.

Dear Lord, guide my steps and protect me from my own
sinful nature. Bring me safely home.

Day 134

The Power of His Precepts

134 Redeem me from the oppression of men,
that I may obey your precepts.

We are all susceptible to the influence of other people. We can be affected by their opinions, their actions, and especially by their criticisms. The psalmist here asks God to be a shield between himself and the people around him.

Your heart may be yearning for God, but it is very hard to resist distractions presented by well-meaning friends:

"Oh, come on, this will be fun. Don't be such a stick-in-the-mud!"

"It's such a beautiful day—why waste it in that stuffy church?"

"I guess you think you're better than me just 'cause you read the Bible!"

How can you resist this kind of pressure? The answer is simple. *You* can't, but *He* can. Turn your every thought to Him. Spend more time with Him in the Bible. Just ask Him, and He will help you resist the temptations of the world.

Dear Lord, I know my friends mean well, but I need
Your help to resist the temptations that they put in my path.

Day 135

The Power of the Light

135 Make your face shine upon your servant
and teach me your decrees.

This verse expresses an age-old yearning for God's light to shine upon us. It is by this light that we can see and understand the Word. It is by this light that we can see the righteous path which we must follow. By the light of the face of God, we can learn and understand His decrees.

Jesus said, "*...I am the light of the world. Whoever follows me will never walk in darkness, but will have the light of life*" (John 8:12). This is a call to wake up and receive the light of Christ. It is a comforting, refreshing, cheering light. It is a soul-satisfying light. Above all, it gives understanding.

God's Spirit hovered over a dark chaos, and brought forth light. His

Spirit can hover over your dark soul, and when the light of God's Word enters it, He brings light to your soul.

Father, let Your face shine down on me and bring
understanding into my mind and heart.

Day 136

The Power of Tears

[136] *Streams of tears flow from my eyes, for your law is not obeyed.*

When you have come to recognize God's great love for this world, and the sacrifice which Jesus made to save the world, then it is very, very hard to watch people reject that love and sacrifice. The world is like a drowning person who struggles against the rescuer who has come to save him.

Jeremiah wept continually for a lost nation. Jesus wept for Jerusalem and its coming destruction. All believers are driven to grief for a world that rejects it's own Rescuer. The more you know God's truth, the more you recognize the tragedy of the actions of unbelievers.

Bendetti, a Franciscan monk, was found weeping one day. When he was asked the reason for his tears, he replied, "I weep because Love goes unloved." Pray for this lost world. Pray that others may find the sweet rescue of a merciful God and the tender comfort of His forgiving arms.

Heavenly Father, I weep for this disobedient world.
Open eyes and ears that are now closed to You and
bring all mankind home to You.

CHAPTER EIGHTEEN
Tzaddi (verses 137-144)

PSALM 119

TZADDI
a Fishhook

MEDITATIONS

Tzaddi, a Fishhook
(pronounced "tzah-dee")

Tzaddi can mean "a trap, a noose, and surrender." The hook is bent, so it is also a symbol of the righteous who are bent in humility. Finally, *tzaddi* represents catching, or hunting for food.

The Old Testament refers to the movement of God's people as their being drawn away on hooks. In Amos 4:2, the people are taken into captivity on fishhooks: *"The Sovereign LORD has sworn by his holiness: The time will surely come when you will be taken away with hooks, the last of you with fishhooks."* In Jeremiah 16:16, they are drawn back the same way: " *'But now I will send for many fishermen,' declares the LORD, 'and they will catch them.'"*

Today, there are anti-Semitic forces coming against Israel with violence and hatred. God will design an attack against these opposing nations and He will do this with fishhooks! *"I will turn you around, put hooks in your jaws and bring you out with your whole army...all of them brandishing their swords"* (Ezekiel 38:4).

The fishhook is truly a tool of God's righteousness.

Psalm 119
Verses 137-144

137   *Righteous are you, O LORD,*
and your laws are right.
138 *The statutes you have laid down are righteous;*
they are fully trustworthy.
139   *My zeal wears me out,*
for my enemies ignore your words.
140 *Your promises have been thoroughly tested,*
and your servant loves them.
141   *Though I am lowly and despised,*
I do not forget your precepts.
142   *Your righteousness is everlasting*
and your law is true.
143 *Trouble and distress have come upon me,*
but your commands are my delight.
144   *Your statutes are forever right;*
give me understanding that I may live.

Hooked on Righteousness

The Psalmist's Heart: A Zeal for Righteousness

The letter *tzaddi* sounds like the Hebrew word for righteousness, which is the keynote for these eight verses. They deal with the perfect righteousness of Jehovah and His Word.

God's righteousness is pure and everlasting. It is the only thing worth pursuing, and the psalmist pursues it with all his heart. Sometimes we are not so anxious for righteousness when its truth condemns us, but the psalmist welcomes being corrected by God's Law. His zeal for the Word is an uplifting example for all believers. It burns in his heart and blazes in his soul.

Your Walk in the Word: Fishing for Souls

Jesus was very much involved with fishing. He chose fishermen for his disciples, and He helped them catch big hauls of fish. He told Peter to cast out a hook to get money to pay his taxes. *"But so that we may not offend them, go to the lake and throw out your line. Take the first fish you catch; open its mouth and you will find a four-drachma coin. Take it and give it to them for my tax and yours"* (Matthew 17:27).

Repeatedly, the Bible tells us that it is the Spirit and the church that draw people into God's net. We are to be used to hook people into the kingdom. Sometimes, we fish with just a pole and hook—talking to one neighbor or friend. Sometimes, we use a big net—television shows and revival meetings. No matter how it's done, be assured that you are doing God's own work: fishing for souls.

Your Walk in the World: Consumed by Zeal

In these verses, the psalmist expresses his zeal for the Word. There are two kinds of zeal: zeal for the Word, and zeal of the world or the flesh. The zeal of the flesh torments men. The zeal of the world causes men to labor day and night just for transitory rewards. A drunkard is consumed with zeal for drinking. A whoremonger is zealous for whoredom. A heretic is eaten up by his zeal for falsehoods. There are no rewards for the zeal of the world.

Zeal of the world consumes the outward man, but zeal for the Word nourishes and refreshes the inward man. Righteous zeal leads to everlasting life.

His Gift for You: Saving Knowledge

If you delight in good things, you tend to be good, and if you delight in evil things, you tend to be evil. Meditation of the Word will save you from earthly cares, and from eternal torment. The saving knowledge of God's testimony is really the only way to live.

Dear God,
Turn my desires away from the world and toward Your life-giving Truth. I long for the understanding that comes only from a zealous heart—a heart hungry and longing for You. I want to be captured in Your net of righteousness, and made into a fisher of men. Use me to shine Your light on the world.

Amen

DEVOTIONS

Day 137

Hooked on God's Judgments

137 Righteous are you, O LORD, and your laws are right.

It isn't often that the Lord's name is used in the Old Testament. Jews believe that His name is sacred, to be used only in worship. They have always considered it disrespectful to overuse it.

The use of the Lord's name in this verse is indicative of the depth of love and adoration that the psalmist is trying to express. It is God's judgments that are exciting such emotion here. His judgments are fearful, because they are consistent and they are always accurate.

Are your prayers always answered just the way you want them to be? When you truly believe in His perfect righteousness, then you will love His judgments even when they cause you pain, or when they are beyond your understanding. Life is only worth living when it is spent in complete trust in the Lord's righteousness.

*Lord, I do not always understand Your answers to my prayers,
but I place all my trust in Your righteous judgment.*

Day 138

Hooked on Trusting Him

*138 The statutes you have laid down are righteous;
they are fully trustworthy.*

Trust is a powerful word. We look for banks we can trust and friends we can trust. It is wonderful that we also have a God we can trust. He is trustworthy, and remains faithful to His promises, even when we do not believe in Him! "*...if we are faithless, he will remain faithful, for he cannot disown himself*" (II Timothy 2:13).

Have you ever gone rock climbing? Climbers literally trust their lives to their climbing companions and the ropes to which they are all tied. It must be very difficult to let go of a rock and trust your very life to that rope!

In the same way, we are called to put our lives in the hands of God. It is hard to let go of controlling our own lives, and to trust God completely. It is important to remember that He has promised to take care of our every need, if we will only let Him. Yes, it is hard, but it is well worth the effort. The reward is peace beyond understanding.

Father, help me to place my life
entirely in Your trustworthy hands.

Day 139

Hooked on a Holy Fire

¹³⁹ *My zeal wears me out,*
for my enemies ignore your words.

Zeal reflects a high degree of love. Grief and indignation can occur when the object of that love is ill-treated. Such zeal can consume the heart. Jesus' heart was consumed with this kind of zeal. When Jesus raged at the money changers and traders in the Temple, *"His disciples remembered that it is written: 'Zeal for your house will consume me' "* (John 2:17).

Zeal is a holy fire which expresses itself in love and anger on God's behalf. True zeal comes from heaven. It is not a fire of hatred, but a spiritual fire of divine love.

Zeal helps you stand firm when your faith is challenged. It gives you strength to endure. How can you fan the flames of zeal in your own heart? Turn to the living Word of God.

"For the word of God is living and active. Sharper than any double-edged sword, it penetrates even to dividing soul and spirit, joints and marrow; it judges the thoughts and attitudes of the heart" (Hebrews 4:12).

Dear God, give me a fire in my
heart for Your commandments.

Day 140

Hooked on Scripture

*140 Your promises have been thoroughly tested,
and your servant loves them.*

The Word is not only pure, it is a purifier. It cleanses us from sin and guilt. Jesus demonstrated this in John 15:3, *"You are already clean because of the word I have spoken to you."*

The Word brings glad tidings to all nations. It holds out the hope of an everlasting kingdom of righteousness and peace. It was given to save sinners. It is the Word of truth: it has no error in it. It is the Word of life: it gives life where there once was death.

Jesus also made it the Word of the Cross. The Word makes us blameless! It is so easy to love the Word, when you consider its power, comfort, and truth.

*Father, I truly love Your Word with all my heart, and I will
dedicate myself to meditating on it all my life.*

Day 141

Hooked on Challenges

*141 Though I am lowly and despised,
I do not forget your precepts.*

The psalmist is beaten down. He is feeling small and powerless. God lets this happen to us so that we may know that our happiness does not come from this world. Experiences like these make us long for something more.

When the provisions of the world are cut off, we become more sensitive to His Laws. We turn against sin and lust, and learn to live on His faithful promises. Hard times teach us to depend only upon God to be our support.

It is times like these that show the enemy there are people who are going to serve God no matter what. They don't serve God just for selfish reasons. One of the most precious gifts that God gives you are these learning experiences.

*Dear Lord, help me to trust and depend on You especially
when I am feeling small and powerless.*

Day 142

Hooked on Eternity

¹⁴² *Your righteousness is everlasting and your law is true.*

Every one of us can behave righteously for a short time, but inevitably, that righteousness comes to an end. God's righteousness is different; it never changes and it never ends.

In this precious verse, the psalmist is feeling small. He is probably surrounded by faithless people who seem to be prospering. It is hard to wait for the rewards of righteousness, especially when others seem to be benefiting from their sins.

At times like these, it is important to remind yourself of the constancy and truthfulness of God's judgment. In His time, not ours, the righteous will be rewarded and sinners will be punished. Hold tight to your obedience to God, even when it doesn't seem to be paying off. Your righteousness is not for today; it is for eternity!

Dear Lord, I long to be an obedient servant to You, even when
there seems to be no short-term rewards.

Day 143

Hooked on the Joy of Christ

¹⁴³ *Trouble and distress have come upon me,*
but your commands are my delight.

Many times, the sweetness of God's Word is best perceived and received under the bitterness of the Cross. The joy of Christ and the joy of the world often appear to be at odds.

If you delight in the world, you lose the consolation of the Spirit. If you delight in the Spirit, you lose a desire for the destructive delights of the world. One negates the other.

How glorious that we have the choice! There really is no comparison between the present life and everlasting life. The present life is a living death, a shadow, a vapor that will quickly disappear.

God, on the other hand, offers eternal life, *"Whoever finds his life will lose it, and whoever loses his life for my sake will find it"* (Matthew 10:39).

Father, I want to live in Christ and take my delight
in the Spirit, not in the world.

Day 144

Hooked on Life

[144] *Your statutes are forever right;*
give me understanding that I may live.

The world provides many different interpretations for what is right, but only the Word gives us the Creator's viewpoint. While every option the world presents leads to confusion, destruction, and death, only God's Word leads us into life.

The psalmist realizes that the more he meditates on God's statutes, the more he experiences the abundant life of God. *"My son, pay attention to what I say; listen closely to my words. Do not let them out of your sight, keep them within your heart; for they are life to those who find them and health to a man's whole body"* (Proverbs 4:20-22).

True life exists only in the recognition and fulfillment of His testimonies. It is obtained only as a gift from God. Eternal life comes from the eternal truths contained in the Word.

Heavenly Father, grant me the understanding
that leads to eternal life.

CHAPTER NINETEEN
Qoph (verses 145-152)

PSALM 119 MEDITATIONS

QOPH
Nape or Back
of the Head

Qoph, Nape or Back of the Head
(pronounced "kohf")

This letter is shaped like the hole in an ax which allows it to be attached to the ax handle. It can mean a "knot" or a "cage," and it can be interpreted as a head with a helmet on it.

The neck of an ax must be made of especially hard wood, because it has to sustain the heavy blows for which it was designed. That part of an ax breaks frequently. Likewise, the juncture of the human head and neck is a focal point of stress—a traffic junction for signals between the brain and other parts of the body. When we engage in challenging activities, we usually protect this critical area by wearing a helmet to provide cushioning and additional support.

It is easy to visualize the Word as *qoph*—a helmet of righteousness that cushions, protects, and sustains the communication that passes from the Head—Jesus Himself—to the Body of Christ. *"But let us, who are of the day, be sober, putting on the breastplate of faith and love; and for a helmet, the hope of salvation"* (I Thessalonians 5:8).

Psalm 119
Verses 145-152

[145] *I call with all my heart; answer me, O LORD,*
and I will obey your decrees.
[146] *I call out to you;*
save me and I will keep your statutes.
[147] *I rise before dawn and cry for help;*
I have put my hope in your word.
[148] *My eyes stay open through the watches*
of the night,
that I may meditate on your promises.
[149] *Hear my voice in accordance with your love;*
preserve my life, O LORD, according to your laws.
[150] *Those who devise wicked schemes are near,*
but they are far from your law.
[151] *Yet you are near, O LORD,*
and all your commands are true.
[152] *Long ago I learned from your statutes*
that you established them to last forever.

Don't Lose Your Head

The Psalmist's Heart: Happy Memories

Hebrew scholars consider *qoph* to represent holiness and growth cycles. Comparing it to an ax handle which can be broken, some scholars say it represents power lost and regained.

The *qoph* verses all concern the psalmist's memories. He remembers times when he lost control of his life, and he remembers God's answers to his pleas in those times. These memories give him confidence to face today's afflictions.

When you pray continually, your faith is strengthened and your hope is continually renewed. The psalmist cherishes this fact, and praises the God Who is so constant.

Your Walk in the Word: The Holy Headship

Jesus is the head and we compose His body. Paul refers to this relationship in Ephesians 4:15-16: *"Instead, speaking the truth in love, we will in all things grow up into him who is the Head, that is, Christ. From him the whole body, joined and held together by every supporting ligament, grows and builds itself up in love, as each part does its work."*

When we walk in His Word, we become a functioning part of His body. Jesus once lamented, *"...Foxes have holes and birds of the air have nests, but the Son of Man has no place to lay his head"* (Matthew 8:20). Was Jesus just looking for a place to take a nap? No, of course not. Jesus sometimes lived with Peter's family, so He had a physical place to rest. In this scripture, He is saddened by the lack of believers who will connect to His headship. Jesus will rest when His body joins Him.

Your Walk in the World: Keep Your Head Attached

Without the neck area, the brain would not be able to communicate with the rest of the body. When there is something wrong with the body, the brain can send out signals to correct the problem. Without *qoph*, your arm could bleed, but the brain would not know to send out blood-clotting signals.

We need *qoph* in our relationship with Jesus, too. We must be connected to Him, the head, in order to stay spiritually healthy. Seek that powerful connection every day, through prayer and meditation. Receive His divine direction in everything you do, say, or think.

His Gift for You: An Eternal Hope

If you have been with God in the closet, you are certainly going to find Him in the furnace. If you cry, you are going to be answered. Delayed answers sometimes spur people to impulsive and misguided actions. Don't lose hope! The ultimate glorious result was found in His Word from the beginning of time.

> *Dear God,*
> *It is the desire of my heart to live forever in the Body of Christ, directed solely by the divine head. Turn my heart toward You, Father. Let me place all my hope and confidence in You, and yield to the direction of Your Word.*
>
> *Amen*

DEVOTIONS

QOPH
Nape or Back
of the Head
MEDITATIONS

Day 145

Don't Lose Your Heart

¹⁴⁵ *I call with all my heart; answer me, O LORD,
and I will obey your decrees.*

In this verse, the psalmist cries out with his whole heart. This is not a prayer said by rote, but a sincere prayer. This verse represents the essence of prayer. God hears every sound that is made on earth—every desire of every heart.

When your prayers are true conversations with God, you feel as if you are talking to a kind and caring physician. You find a friendly ear that hears and truly understands your pleas.

We pray most effectively with a whole heart. The most heartfelt prayers are not requests for earthly things, but expressions of affection for God. It's fine to pray for physical needs, but those things will rust, decay, and perish. God will meet those requests, but He is more concerned with what is in your heart.

"My son, give me your heart..." (Proverbs 23:26).

> *Father, I give You my whole heart–I love
> You above everything in this world.*

Day 146

Don't Lose Your Intensity

¹⁴⁶ *I call out to you; Save me and I will keep your statutes.*

This psalmist calls out to God. There is no other source of power, comfort, or hope. The psalmist prays to be saved, but he knows that there's no saving a man who abides in disobedience and ignorance. If you are immersed in God's Word, your prayers will flow from your heart to His.

The entire nation of Israel cried out to God at the banks of the Red Sea, and God gave them a great miracle. The men of the Reformation prayed earnestly and constantly. Luther spent long nights in loud prayer. John Welch went into his garden night after night crying to the Lord to give him Scotland.

God hears what the heart speaks. If the heart is dumb, God will be deaf. The speaking of a prayer is not as important as the frame of the spirit. The prayers which touch God's heart are those which call out from the depths of your heart. A crying prayer pierces the heights of heaven.

Father, don't let my heart be dumb. Hear the prayers of my heart.

Day 147

Don't Lose the Precious Morning Hour

147 I rise before dawn and cry for help;
I have put my hope in your word.

For the third day in a row, the psalmist cries. It is interesting that he cries three times in this psalm. Jesus prayed three times in the Garden of Gethsemane (Matthew 26:44). Paul prayed three times to have the thorn in his flesh removed (II Corinthians 12:8). Elijah stretched himself out on the dead child three times in order to bring him back to life (I Kings 17:21).

The Word continues to give us hope. If you are diligent in prayer, you will never be destitute of hope. Just as the early bird gets the worm, early morning prayer, undisturbed by the cares and agitations of life, is especially precious and fruitful.

Start each day in communion with God, and you will be amazed at how His comfort surrounds you throughout your day.

Dear God, help me to wake early so that I can
spend that precious time with You.

Day 148

Don't Lose a Minute

148 My eyes stay open through the watches of the night,
that I may meditate on your promises.

In the last verse, we were reminded of the importance of starting our day in prayer. Now the psalmist also claims the nighttime for God. The Jews, like the Greeks and Romans, divided the night into military watches instead of hours. Each of three watches represented a period that sentinels remained on duty.

There was the beginning watch: *"Arise, cry out in the night, as the watches of the night begin; pour out your heart like water in the presence of the Lord..."* (Lamentations 2:19); the middle watch: *"Gideon and the hundred men with him reached the edge of the camp at the beginning of the middle watch, just after they had changed the guard. They blew their trumpets and broke the jars that were in their hands"* (Judges 7:19); and the morning watch: *"During the last watch of the night the LORD looked down from the pillar of fire and cloud at the Egyptian army and threw it into confusion"* (Exodus 14:24).

The soldiers changed guards, but the psalmist did not change his occupation: he kept praying. Prayer is a fruitful activity at any time of day or night!

Father, turn my heart to prayer from morning to night.

Day 149

Don't Lose Your Life

¹⁴⁹ *Hear my voice in accordance with your love;*
    preserve my life, O LORD, according to your laws.

God, being righteous, must obey the laws of His moral universe. In this verse, the psalmist calls upon God to follow two of these laws.

In the first line, God hears our voices, not because we deserve to be heard, but because He loves us. Because His love is perfect, He hears us even with all our imperfections and failings. All of our prayers are unworthy of such a God, yet He listens and answers out of divine love.

In the second line, we are reassured that we can expect an answer to our prayers simply because God's Word promises that He will answer. *"If you believe, you will receive whatever you ask for in prayer"* (Matthew 21:22). Not only are you assured of an answer to every prayer, but you can be assured that every answer will preserve your life. He will answer out of His wisdom and righteousness.

Dear Lord, hear my prayers and answer according
to Your will and wisdom.

Day 150

Don't Lose Your Cool

*150 Those who devise wicked schemes are near,
but they are far from your law.*

The psalmist hears the footfall of the enemy behind him. He hears their dreaded approach. They are far from the Law because the wicked life cannot be an obedient one. This is a consistent Law of God.

It is frightening to be threatened by those who have no knowledge of God. Such people have no boundaries and no hope. They are the most dangerous people, because their distance from the Law gives them the liberty to do harm.

Time spent with the Word, from early morning and into the night, keeps us close to God's Law, and creates more distance between us and the schemes of the wicked.

*Dear Lord, help me keep distance from
those who devise wicked schemes.*

Day 151

Don't Lose Your Key

*151 Yet you are near, O LORD,
and all your commands are true.*

In the last verse, the wicked were far from the Law. This verse reminds us that no matter how close danger and temptation from the enemy may seem, God is closer. He is always nearby, just waiting for us to call on Him. God's commands never change and never fail. They are the shield which He has provided to protect us from evil. They are the key to overcoming fear and temptation.

It is a great comfort, when you are under attack, to know that the Lord is near to hear your cries and offer speedy assistance. It is awesome to be able to call on an unchangeable God to keep His neverfailing and unbreakable promise!

If only wicked schemers realized that God is close to them, too, then they might abandon their wicked schemes and turn to Him!

*Father, thank You for always being near.
Help my enemies to turn toward You!*

Day 152

Don't Lose Your Perspective

*152 Long ago I learned from your statutes
that you established them to last forever.*

Our God is a prayer-hearing, promise-keeping, sin-forgiving God. He has always been a covenant-keeping God and a gracious, tender Father. The world and its riches and fashion pass away, but God is unchangeable.

The more you meditate upon His statutes, the more you delight in His consistency. He is the same in the beginning, now, and evermore.

What is worrying you today? Consider the scope of those worries against the span of eternity. Your worries are just for today, but God's Law is forever. Set aside your passing problems, and spend time in the eternal Word. Be comforted that He has all of your troubles under control. He anticipated every one of them before you were ever born, and He takes care of you today and tomorrow just as He always has.

He is asking you right now to let Him carry your burdens, while you flood your mind and your heart with His Word.

*Heavenly Father, I lay down my temporary worries,
and take up Your eternal Word.*

CHAPTER TWENTY
Resh (verses 153-160)

Resh, the First
(pronounced "reysh")

Resh refers not only to the physical head, but also to time and rank. It is the beginning and the end. It is the commander, ruler, or head of state. *Resh* can also represent a cornerstone, the top of a mountain, the firstborn, the firstfruits, or the first in line.

Hebrew scholars see *resh* as the Holy One—the head of all creation and the beginning and end of everything. The head or first is Jesus Christ: *"And he is the head of the body, the church; he is the beginning and the firstborn from among the dead, so that in everything he might have the supremacy"* (Colossians 1:18).

Psalm 119
Verses 153-160

153   *Look upon my suffering and deliver me,*
   for I have not forgotten your law.
   154   *Defend my cause and redeem me;*
preserve my life according to your promise.
   155   *Salvation is far from the wicked,*
   for they do not seek out your decrees.
   156   *Your compassion is great, O LORD;*
preserve my life according to your laws.
   157   *Many are the foes who persecute me,*
but I have not turned from your statutes.
   158   *I look on the faithless with loathing,*
   for they do not obey your word.
   159   *See how I love your precepts;*
   preserve my life, O LORD,
   according to your love.
   160   *All your words are true;*
all your righteous laws are eternal.

Rule Over Your Enemies

The Psalmist's Heart: Nearer to God

In this octave, the psalmist expresses a desire to come closer and closer to God. He devotes his every thought and action to this goal, and places all his hope in His Word.

He relies on God to show him the right path and to give him the stamina to walk upon that path. He seeks people who love the Lord as he does, and he grieves at how many of those around him do not love or obey the Word.

Danger and suffering will not sway him from his resolution. He realizes that afflictions have made him better and more obedient.

Your Walk in the Word: Jesus' Many Titles

Every designation for *resh* can be found in the Bible as a title for Jesus Christ.

• He is the cornerstone:

"For in Scripture it says: 'See, I lay a stone in Zion, a chosen and precious cornerstone, and the one who trusts in him will never be put to shame'" (I Peter 2:6).

"Jesus looked directly at them and asked, 'Then what is the meaning of that which is written: 'The stone the builders rejected has become the capstone'?" (Luke 20:17).

• He is the head of the church:

"And he is the head of the body, the church; he is the beginning and the firstborn from among the dead, so that in everything he might have the supremacy" (Colossians 1:18).

"For the husband is the head of the wife as Christ is the head of the church, his body, of which he is the Savior" (Ephesians 5:23).

• He is the firstborn:

"And again, when God brings his firstborn into the world, he says, 'Let all God's angels worship him' " (Hebrews 1:6).

• He is the commander:

"For it became him, for whom are all things, and by whom are all things, in bringing many sons unto glory, to make the captain of their salvation perfect through sufferings" (Hebrews 2:10 KJV)

• He is the supreme ruler:

"But you, Bethlehem Ephrathah, though you are small among the clans of Judah, out of you will come for me one who will be ruler over Israel, whose origins are from of old, from ancient times" (Micah 5:2).

"He will be great and will be called the Son of the Most High. The Lord God will give him the throne of his father David," (Luke 1:32).

• He is the firstfruits:

"But Christ has indeed been raised from the dead, the firstfruits of those who have fallen asleep" (I Corinthians 15:20).

• He is the beginning and the end:

"When I saw him, I fell at his feet as though dead. Then he placed his right hand on me and said: 'Do not be afraid. I am the First and the Last . . . '" (Revelation 1:17).

Your Walk in the World: The Only God

As believers we feel rather lonely in this world. How wonderful it is to know that someday the entire world, all the nations, every voice will worship our God!

"Therefore God exalted him to the highest place and gave him the name that is above every name, that at the name of Jesus every knee should bow, in heaven and on earth and under the earth, and every tongue confess that Jesus Christ is Lord, to the glory of God the Father" (Philippians 2:9-11).

His Gift for You: Cherished by the Ruler

Your God is constant and eternal. He is not going to change or disappear. You can count on Him forever, and someday you will experience the ecstasy of seeing Him praised and worshipped by all of creation!

Dear God,
I praise You as the one eternal God. You are the one Who rules the heavens and earth; You are the cornerstone; You are the head of the body; You are the first and last, the beginning and the end. It is almost unimaginable that One so great could care for me. You hold me secure in Your arms, You cherish me, and I love Your name!

Amen

DEVOTIONS

Day 153

Rule Over Suffering

153   Look upon my suffering and deliver me,
for I have not forgotten your law.

The psalmist states his case and invokes divine help with boldness and expectation. His prayer to God is one that could benefit all of us, "God, look at my suffering and bear my burden, pay my price, bring me out to liberty." That is a mighty plea, based on the Word. There isn't a weapon in any arsenal that can match that.

God looks upon man in different ways for different purposes:

- To heal him: *"As he went along, he saw a man blind from birth"* (John 9:1).
- To convert him: *"...he saw a man named Matthew sitting at the tax collector's booth. 'Follow me,' he told him, and Matthew got up and followed him"* (Matthew 9:9).
- To deliver him: *"The LORD said, 'I have indeed seen the misery of my people in Egypt...and I am concerned about their suffering' "* (Exodus 3:7).
- To reward him: *"...The LORD looked with favor on Abel and his offering,"* (Genesis 4:4).

Father, look upon me and stand in my stead.
Bring me out to liberty.

Day 154

Rule Over Your Natural Self

154   Defend my cause and redeem me;
preserve my life according to your promise.

Often, when we are in trouble, we trust too much in our own wits.

We lean on our own inventions. We trade one evil device for another. We don't commit our cause to God.

In this verse, the psalmist turns to God for his defense. He asks God to redeem him. God claims that vengeance is His: *"Dearly beloved, avenge not yourselves, but rather give place unto wrath: for it is written, Vengeance is mine; I will repay, saith the Lord"* (Romans 12:19 KJV). We are instructed to believe in the supernatural deliverance of God.

After turning his cause over to God, the psalmist seeks his godly pearl: God will preserve his life. It is so comforting to find God's blessings in every circumstance. After all, what earthly circumstance can compare to the fact that Jesus came to give us life, and that more abundantly (John 10:10 KJV)?

Lord, I turn over to You the job of
defending me and preserving my life.

Day 155

Rule Over Disobedience

¹⁵⁵ *Salvation is far from the wicked,*
for they do not seek out your decrees.

The desires for obedience and salvation are inseparable. If you are saved, you long to obey. You will seek out His decrees. You will have an appetite for the Word. Those who reject His Word are separated from salvation by their own disobedience.

God longs for our obedience for two reasons: we will be saved, and He will be glorified. This does not mean you will lose your salvation if you slip up just once. God knows you cannot be perfect. Your disobedience, no matter how small, hurts Him as much as it hurts you. He grieves, but He also understands.

The great miracle is that He knew you were going to make that mistake before you ever made it, and He sent His Son to pay your penalty. Can there be any greater proof of His love for you? Doesn't such divine love just make you yearn with all your heart to know and obey Him?

Dear God, guide me so that I may
obey You with all my heart.

Day 156

Rule With Mercy

156 Your compassion is great, O LORD;
preserve my life according to your laws.

God's mercy is both great and tender. It is great in its consistency (it never changes), its endurance (it will be forever), and its scope (it reaches into heaven). God's mercy transcends all the works of God.

At the same time, His mercies are tender. The Lord is easy to approach and slow to anger. James says, *"But the wisdom that is from above is first pure, then peaceable, gentle, and easy to be intreated, full of mercy and good fruits, without partiality, and without hypocrisy"* (James 3:17 KJV). Jesus told us to forgive 70 times 7, and He forgives us just as freely.

How could we ask anything more of our master and our king? He showers us with mercy that is both great and tender—an exquisite combination! The more you understand God's divine character, the more you long to become like Him.

Father, teach me to be merciful as You are merciful.

Day 157

Rule Over the World

157 Many are the foes who persecute me,
but I have not turned from your statutes.

Again, the psalmist praises God's compassion for the righteous. Faithfulness to the truth is really our best and only victory over our enemies.

When the world attacks, it is our natural inclination to turn away from God and His Word. Sometimes, we are bitter or blame God for our troubles. Sometimes, we are so preoccupied with trying to solve problems on our own that we neglect God. Living in the natural causes us to turn away from the supernatural, even though the natural world offers no real answers or solutions.

It is important, when you suffer persecution, to cling steadfastly to God's Word. Only He can defend you against your enemies, and only He can comfort you when you are grieving. Don't turn away from Him. Instead, run with all your heart and strength into His compassionate arms.

Dear Lord, I need to rest in Your mercy and the wonderful
promises of Your Word.

Day 158

Rule Over Hatred

158 *I look on the faithless with loathing,*
for they do not obey your word.

It is so sad to see sinners! The hurt that they inflict on others is nothing compared to the hurt they inflict on themselves. The real tragedy is their faithlessness to the God Who loves them and longs to forgive them.

Such ingratitude is repulsive to those who love God. When you are confronted by those who mock God, it is important to strive to emulate Jesus' compassion and God's great mercy. It is easy to hate evil. It is not so easy to love and to forgive those who do evil things. The believer lives not by the Word alone, but also by the mercy that goes with the Word.

Dear Lord, in my anger against those who mock You,
let me also reflect Your compassionate spirit.

Day 159

Rule Over Betrayal

159 *See how I love your precepts; preserve my life, O LORD,*
according to your love.

Once again, the psalmist asks God to look upon his devotion, and preserve his life. The psalmist does not just read the Word, but loves to learn it, think upon it, proclaim it, and most of all, put it into practice. Because of his dedication to the Word, the psalmist trusts God's promise of protection and deliverance.

God's commands are easy to love! God gave them to us because He loves us and wants the very best for us. It can be difficult to live each command daily, but they are so excellent that it is a joy to love and honor them.

Whenever our natural selves are disobedient, the result is a deep sadness at betraying the greatest gift of God. When we keep our focus on the Word, then the resulting obedience is a source of great joy and gladness.

Seek to follow Him, and He will give you an obedient heart. Because God is love, He gives you life. Because He is kind, He will rekindle the heavenly flame within you.

Father, I love Your Word. I long for an obedient heart.

Day 160

Rule With Truth

[160] All your words are true;
all your righteous laws are eternal.

From the beginning, God's Word has been true. We need to trust His Word. The truth of the Word is a wonderful gift.

It sets you free. *"Then you will know the truth, and the truth will set you free"* (John 8:32).

It lives in you. *"And I will ask the Father, and he will give you another Counselor to be with you forever—the Spirit of truth...he lives with you and will be in you"* (John 14:16,17)

It is a weapon against evil. *"Stand firm then, with the belt of truth buckled around your waist,..."* (Ephesians 6:14).

It is your birthright. *"He chose to give us birth through the word of truth,..."* (James 1:18).

The Bible is the written Word and Jesus is the living Word. Cherish the One Who is truth.

Heavenly Father, I worship Your
eternal truth which is my salvation.

CHAPTER TWENTY-ONE
Shin (verses 161-168)

PSALM 119 MEDITATIONS

SHIN
the Tooth

Shin or Sin, the Tooth, or to Digest
(pronounced "sheen" or "seen")

Shin and *sin* are look-alike letters. The only difference is the dot placed above the crown. If the dot is on the left, the letter is *sin,* and if it is on the right it is *shin.*

The shape of the letter resembles a molar, the grinding tooth. Hebrew scholars associate this letter with digesting the Word of God. It also refers to craggy "saw-tooth" mountains. An alternative name for Mount Sinai is Harbashan which means "a mountain with teeth." From this mountain, Moses brought the truth of God's Law to the Israelites.

Finally, *shin* means "hardness." Teeth are made of hard material, and they are imbedded in the jaw with roots to give them strength.

Psalm 119
Verses 161-168

[161] Rulers persecute me without cause,
but my heart trembles at your word.
[162] I rejoice in your promise
like one who finds great spoil.
[163] I hate and abhor falsehood
but I love your law.
[164] Seven times a day I praise you
for your righteous laws.
[165] Great peace have they who love your law,
and nothing can make them stumble.
[166] I wait for your salvation, O LORD,
and I follow your commands.
[167] I obey your statutes,
for I love them greatly.
[168] I obey your precepts and your statutes,
for all my ways are known to you.

Sink Your Teeth Into the Truth

The Psalmist's Heart: Digest the Word

The psalmist understood that we must have a keen edge, sharpened on the Word. Reading and meditating upon the Word gives us "teeth" of spiritual wisdom.

We must chew up and fully digest the truth that God has revealed. It hardens us and makes us strong so that we can withstand the attacks of the enemy. The roots of the Word must be embedded deep in our hearts so that they cannot be dislodged by temptations or distractions from the natural world.

Your Walk in the Word: God's Strength

Teeth can be used by evil men to bite and devour. Tormented men gnash their teeth. The prophets, on the other hand, delivered messages with a strong "bite." Jesus' message was clear and immovable. *"They went to Capernaum, and when the Sabbath came, Jesus went into the synagogue and began to teach. The people were amazed at his teaching, because he taught them as one who had authority, not as the teachers of the law"* (Mark 1:21,22).

God promised that he would give tiny Israel great strength. *"See, I will make you into a threshing sledge, new and sharp, with many teeth. You will thresh the mountains and crush them, and reduce the hills to chaff"* (Isaiah 41:15). That strength comes through the careful study and heartfelt meditation on the Word of God. When we fully chew it, swallow it, and digest it, the Word nourishes us and makes us strong.

Your Walk in the World: The Strength of Forgiveness

Jesus used His mouth to speak correction and healing. While He hung on the cross, the men who were crucified with Him cast the same taunts in His teeth: *"The thieves also, which were crucified with him, cast the same in his teeth"* (Matthew 27:44 KJV).

Even so, He did not seek revenge. Instead, he reached out with love and assistance. *"Then he said, 'Jesus, remember me when you come into your kingdom.' Jesus answered him, 'I tell you the truth, today you will be with me in paradise'"* (Luke 23:42,43).

Strength does not mean the power to destroy your enemies. Spiritual strength is the ability to love and forgive those who mock and hurt you.

His Gift for You: A Message With Teeth

God was truth even before He created the world. He set down His truth for us in His holy Word. That truth may not always be popular or easy, but it is eternally true!

Dear God,
I am so grateful that You are a God Who speaks in truth and strength. Though I may rebel from time to time, I love Your Word and long to chew on it and digest it for all my life. I know that Your truth nourishes me, while the lies of the world can only decay me. Keep my heart and mind focused on Your Word.

Amen

DEVOTIONS

Day 161

Sink Your Teeth Into a Higher Power

*161   Rulers persecute me without cause,
but my heart trembles at your word.*

We expect our government to be fair and righteous. Rulers are supposed to protect the innocent and avenge the oppressed. It is frightening when institutions designed to protect turn to persecution.

Jesus told us to render homage to the kings of the earth (Matthew 22:21). When John the Baptist talked to the Roman soldiers, he didn't tell them to rebel. He told them to quit complaining about their pay and do violence to no man (Luke 3:14).

We are subject to higher powers, but we are meant to render fear only to the One to Whom fear is due. *"For rulers hold no terror for those who do right, but for those who do wrong. Do you want to be free from fear of the one in authority? Then do what is right and he will commend you"* (Romans 13:3).

Father, I am so glad that I am ruled by a perfect and just king.

Day 162

Sink Your Teeth Into Joy

162   I rejoice in your promise like one who finds great spoil.

We come to God in fear and trembling, yet we experience great joy in His presence. The fear of God is not the kind of fear which perfect love casts out (I John 4:18). The fear of God is the kind of fear which nourishes.

The psalmist compares his joy to one who has been in battle a long time and at last wins the victory and divides the spoils. Now, the uncertainty is over and there is a sense of security. The enemy's been defeated and peace reigns. It is a wonderful time!

The profits of searching the scriptures are greater than any trophies of war. The fight for divine truth is a real battle, by which we gain something precious.

At other times, we simply stumble upon spiritual truth. Whether you are a finder or a warrior, the Word is equally dear.

Lord, Your Word is so precious to me—it
brings me unspeakable joy!

Day 163

Sink Your Teeth Into Right Teachings

163 *I hate and abhor falsehood but I love your law.*

If you're walking in the Spirit, you love truth and you hate lying.

Lying comes from the devil, and leads to the devil. We hate lying because it is degrading, and it is dangerous.

We love the Word because it is productive and constructive. The Word comes from God and leads to God.

The Law of God is truth, and if you love God you hate anything that distorts His character. Be particularly careful to reject false doctrine. *"'Indeed, I am against those who prophesy false dreams,' declares the LORD. 'They tell them and lead my people astray with their reckless lies, yet I did not send or appoint them. They do not benefit these people in the least,' declares the LORD"* (Jeremiah 23:32).

Solomon, the richest and wisest king in all history, asked God for his daily bread, but his more urgent request was, *"Keep falsehood and lies far from me;..."* (Proverbs 30:8).

Dear God, lead me in truth, and guard my heart
from the lies of false prophets.

Day 164

Sink Your Teeth Into Praise

164 *Seven times a day I praise you for your righteous laws.*

The Hebrews are accustomed to praising God seven times a day: twice in the morning before reading the Ten Commandments, and once after, then twice in the evening before reading the same portion of inspiration, and twice after.

Seven is the number of perfection. Most of us do not make the time to praise God seven times a day. Sadly, some of us only praise him once in seven days. True praise is continual, even 70 times 7 times a day! Singing praise to God should be done joyfully, not as a duty. True praise is not tiring, it is energizing.

These praise times are peaceful and encouraging. There is great peace in loving the Lord. The more we forsake the offenses of men, the more we get into the heart of God. Resolve now to praise God seven times a day or more, and see what a grand difference it can make in your life.

Father, I want to praise You all the day!

Day 165

Sink Your Teeth Into Peace

[165] *Great peace have they who love your law,*
and nothing can make them stumble.

The world is full of stress. There are stress-management institutes, stress-management drugs, and stress-management exercises. How frazzled and worried is this lost world!

Thankfully, *we* have another answer. The only real peace comes from loving the Word of God. The Word does more than calm your mind. The Hebrew word for peace is *shalom* which means "perfection, holiness, prosperity, tranquillity, most wholesome, safety, completion, and consummation of every good thing." Shalom is really a blessing, asking that all may be prosperous with you.

God is the God of peace. *"Peace I leave with you; my peace I give you. I do not give to you as the world gives. Do not let your hearts be troubled and do not be afraid"* (John 14:27). No, we don't need biofeedback or drugs—we have the precious Word!

Dear Lord, fill my heart with Your heavenly peace.

Day 166

Sink Your Teeth Into Salvation

166 *I wait for your salvation, O LORD,*
and I follow your commands.

In times of trouble, there are just two things to be done. First, hope in God. Second, do that which is right.

The psalmist glories in God's salvation. In spite of the persecution which his beliefs have brought upon him, he is not ashamed. He is not ashamed of his own actions, and he is not ashamed of his God.

When you are absorbed in the Word, you are content to peacefully wait for His salvation. No taunts or insults from the world can hurt you. You calmly proclaim the righteousness of God. No one can hurt your feelings, because you are following your faithful and compassionate Lord.

What a glorious sacred circle: your faith leads you to obey and your obedience leads you to believe. As you draw nearer to God, He draws you nearer to Him.

Dear Lord, I am not ashamed of my faith.
I rest secure in Your gift of salvation.

Day 167

Sink Your Teeth Into God's Word

167 *I obey your statutes, for I love them greatly.*

God's statutes are beautiful jewels, much more precious than any stones at the finest jewelers. God's statutes are rare; there are none like them. They are valuable: no earthly price can be placed on them. God's statutes beautify those who wear them. Their glitter lights the darkness.

When you possess diamonds and rubies, you must have a special storage place for security. Divine jewels also need to be stored in a receptacle designed just for them: your soul. Only there can they shine and demonstrate their great value.

To keep those precious jewels in your soul, you need a special lock. That lock is your love for them. If you love the Word and hide it in your heart, it can never be stolen from you. Loving the Word protects you from the thieves of the world who continually try to steal your treasure.

Father, my love for Your Word locks its treasure forever in my heart.

208

Day 168

Sink Your Teeth Into Obedience

> [168] *I obey your precepts and your statutes,*
> *for all my ways are known to you.*

The psalmist wants to be right in his heart and his head. His outward life follows God's statutes; his inward life stores up His precepts.

The word *obey* here also means "keep" as in keeping a prisoner, or keeping one's life. The precepts are to be kept carefully, diligently, studiously, and exactly.

All our ways are set before the Lord. He sees everything. You are never hidden from His eye. He is not looking for perfection from you, but He does want your sincerity. Do you sincerely wish to obey Him? He wants to help!

Willingly lay everything before Him: your obedience and your disobedience. The light of His eyes will inspire you to greater and greater obedience and to ever-increasing joy.

> *Heavenly Father, look at all I am and all I do,*
> *and shine Your light of truth on my life.*

CHAPTER TWENTY-TWO
Tau (verses 169-176)

Tau, a Cross-Shaped Mark or Sign
(pronounced "tahv")

Tau can be "a mark, a signature, a brand, or a sign." The first person in the Bible to be marked was Cain. God himself put the mark of *tau* on Cain's head to protect him. God told Ezekiel to put a *tau* on the forehead of the righteous. *"...Go throughout the city of Jerusalem and put a mark on the foreheads of those who grieve and lament over all the detestable things that are done in it"* (Ezekiel 9:4). The mark of *tau* spared those people from judgment.

Just as livestock are branded so that herders may identify them, so too are God's people branded as the sheep of His flock. The faithful were marked by Ezekiel for their protection. Cain was marked for his protection. God's mark is a saving mark.

The mark of the Cross, of course, is the symbol of the ultimate sacrifice which Jesus made for us. The Cross will forever be the mark of unselfish love and salvation.

Psalm 119
Verses 169-176

169   *May my cry come before you, O LORD;*
give me understanding according to your word.
170   *May my supplication come before you;*
deliver me according to your promise.
171   *May my lips overflow with praise,*
for you teach me your decrees.
172   *May my tongue sing of your word,*
for all your commands are righteous.
173   *May your hand be ready to help me,*
for I have chosen your precepts.
174   *I long for your salvation, O LORD,*
and your law is my delight.
175   *Let me live that I may praise you,*
and may your laws sustain me.
176   *I have strayed like a lost sheep.*
Seek your servant, for I have not
forgotten your commands.

Make Your Mark

The Psalmist's Heart: Marking God's People

The Jews were the most God-marked people upon the earth. They made a point of wearing clothing that marked them as different from other men. They used specific, visual rituals in their worship. They ate different foods. God set out certain holidays, such as the Sabbath and Passover, as a sign of His covenant with them. Circumcision was a token of the contract between God and the Jewish people.

Only God could mark His people. The Israelites were not to put any kind of mark or tattoo on their bodies. The mark of *tau* was a signature of good faith, an assurance of God's promises.

Your Walk in the Word: A Circumcised Heart

Just as circumcision of the flesh was the mark of the Old Testament, circumcision of the heart is the mark of the New Testament believer.

"The LORD your God will circumcise your hearts and the hearts of your descendants, so that you may love him with all your heart and with all your soul, and live" (Deuteronomy 30:6).

"A man is not a Jew if he is only one outwardly, nor is circumcision merely outward and physical. No, a man is a Jew if he is one inwardly; and circumcision is circumcision of the heart, by the Spirit, not by the written code. Such a man's praise is not from men, but from God" (Romans 2:28,29).

When we symbolically circumcise our hearts, we are open to receive the love of God, and are marked as His people forevermore.

Your Walk in the World: The Mark of Love

Jesus declares that men would recognize us as His disciples by our genuine love and compassion: *"By this shall all men know that you are my disciples, if ye have love one to another"* (John 13:35). These are marks of a godly person. When worldly people look at you, do they see God's love? The true mark of the Cross is mercy, forgiveness, and kindness. Carry the mark of the godly with you into the world!

His Gift for You: Marked by God

When you were saved, you were marked as God's own child. That mark is eternal. It identifies you as His heir with Jesus. You are marked for a sure place in the grandest kingdom that earth and heaven have ever seen.

Dear God,
Thank You that I am marked as your child. Let me reflect You in my thoughts and actions, so that even the ungodly will see Your mark, and they will come to delight in You, too.

Amen

DEVOTIONS

PSALM 119

TAU
a Cross-Shaped
Mark or Sign

MEDITATIONS

Day 169

The Mark of an Heir

> *169 May my cry come before you, O LORD;*
> *give me understanding according to your word.*

Prayer is such a glorious privilege! Though we are confined to earth, our prayers rise past the very seraphim to come before God!

When you speak before people of power, you have to watch your manners very carefully. You would never try to tell a judge in a courtroom how to do his job, or to remind a tax agent of the law. It's different when we speak with God.

When our prayers come before God, Who is much more powerful than any judge, we can speak with him as a friend. Because we know His Word is perfect truth, we can remind Him again and again of His own laws. We can petition him repeatedly, because we are His children. When we pray, we are being admitted to His most royal court. The King, who could easily condemn us for our many sins, instead greets us as the heirs to His kingdom!

> *Father, I bow down before you, the most powerful King,*
> *Who has adopted me as Your own.*

Day 170

The Mark of Prayer

> *170 May my supplication come before you;*
> *deliver me according to your promise.*

In this verse, the psalmist begs God to hear his prayers. We are not content with anything short of a personal relationship with God. We must have it. It is the innermost longing of every human being, and can only be satisfied by heartfelt communion with God.

With each sincere prayer we raise, we praise God and call for Him to come close and look upon us. He has promised us a close relationship, and our dedication to His Word reminds Him of that promise.

It is easier to communicate with someone you know well than with a stranger. When you read and meditate upon God's Word, you are getting to know Him better and better. You become more intimate with Him, and you become more and more like Him. Your prayers fly up to your best friend, Who will answer with infinite love and wisdom.

Lord, my conversations with You are so precious to me!

Day 171

The Mark of the Teacher

171 *May my lips overflow with praise,*
for you teach me your decrees.

If your life honors the Lord, you are going to be a person of praise. When you seek God with all your heart, His Word teaches you how to praise Him. Praise will flow out of your mouth without any conscious effort on your part. In fact, you can't prevent it!

The more He teaches you, the more you appreciate Him. The lessons He leads you through serve to prove over and over how faithful He really is. Your heart will overflow with thankfulness for such a loving God.

Sometimes, your lessons are hard, and even painful. He teaches you because He loves you, and you love Him because He teaches you. Seek His lessons with all your heart—and your heart will be the benefactor. Learn and praise; praise and learn. It is a splendid education!

Dear God, teach me so that my heart
will overflow with praise for You.

Day 172

The Mark of the Preacher

172 *May my tongue sing of your word,*
for all your commands are righteous.

In this verse, the psalmist moves from praising to preaching. He asks God to guide his tongue, so that God's Word can be truthfully expressed.

All believers should strive to become orators for God. Every word that comes from our mouths should be placed there by God. When Moses told God that he could not be a public speaker, *"The LORD said to him, 'Who gave man his mouth? Who makes him deaf or mute? Who gives him sight or makes him blind? Is it not I, the LORD? Now go; I will help you speak and will teach you what to say' "* (Exodus 4:11,12).

Every time you open your mouth, first pray that God will give you the right words. Whether you are speaking to just one friend or to an auditorium full of people, let God do the talking.

Father, let the words of my lips be Yours and
continually reflect only Your truth.

Day 173

The Mark of the Helping Hand

> [173] *May your hand be ready to help me,*
> *for I have chosen your precepts.*

We all need God's hand to guide us through the storms of life. When Peter was walking on the water and began to sink, he cried out, "Lord, save me!" (Matthew 14:30). The Lord stretched His hand out for Peter's rescue, and He will reach to you when you cry out, too.

When we stray from the path, we begin to lose ourselves. Like a lost sheep, we stray further and further from home, without even realizing it. Remember, no matter how far you have wandered, you are still His sheep and He is still your shepherd. You need only call out, and the shepherd will rush to your aid.

Everyone longs to find the way home. Turn to God's Word and you will find it is the road map the shepherd has prepared to guide you back to His love and protection.

Dear Lord, guide me back home when I wander.

Day 174

The Mark of Duty

174 I long for your salvation, O LORD,
and your law is my delight.

There are things we pray and things we do. Here, the psalmist prays for salvation, and he delights in the Word. A duty always accompanies an answered prayer.

God delivered Noah from the flood, but Noah moved with reverence to prepare the ark (Genesis 6:22). God saved Lot from Sodom, but Lot was commanded to get out quickly and not look back (Genesis 19:17). God was pleased to cure Hezekiah of the plague, but Hezekiah had to take a lump of figs and lay it on his boil (Isaiah 38:21). God promised Paul safety when his ship was about to be wrecked, but the sailors had to stay on the ship to be saved (Acts 27:31).

The more you receive of God's Word, the more you desire Him. Your duties become your greatest joy!

Dear Lord, show me what You want me to do,
for I want to be closer and closer to You.

Day 175

The Mark of the Cross

175 Let me live that I may praise you,
and may your laws sustain me.

Spiritual life is eternal, and our purpose is to praise God. Never are we completely fulfilled except when praising God.

When we live in the Word, our lives produce more and more praise for God Who directs us. This praise strengthens our spiritual lives, so that they reflect more of God's righteousness.

The life-giving experience of the Cross reconciles us to God. It is the mark of our protection and covenant. We belong to Him because He purchased us with His blood on the Cross. The Cross is the proof that He keeps His promises. It is the sign that He is faithful in everything.

Because of His sacrifice on the Cross, we praise Him eternally, from the depths of our hearts.

Father, how I praise Your name for the precious gift of Your Son
and His astonishing sacrifice on the Cross.

Day 176

The Mark of the Sheep

[176] *I have strayed like a lost sheep.*
Seek your servant, for I have not forgotten your commands.

How wonderful it is to know that we have been branded for all eternity as God's beloved sheep! No matter where we wander or how we might stray, He will seek us out and return us to His shelter.

As long as we remember His promises, He will remember us. The shepherd always recognizes His brand on your heart, and He will claim you as His own.

It is breathtaking to consider that we are chosen by Him to live with Him forever in His perfect and righteous kingdom. We serve an awesome God, and it is the greatest privilege to spend our days praising Him for His greatness. What a stunning God we serve!

Heavenly Father, let me never forget Your commands,
for I long to serve You forever.

CHAPTER TWENTY-THREE

PSALM 119 MEDITATIONS

Meditating On and Memorizing the Word

by Sarah Bowling

Meditation:
Your Key to Intimacy With God

Meditation is a major key to spiritual growth. If you desire to develop into the strong man or woman of God that He has called you to be, it is crucial that you learn how to meditate in the Word of God.

Let's talk about meditating so that we are on common ground. It will be helpful, first, to understand what godly meditating **is not**.

Meditating on God's Word *is not*:
- an "escape" from one's circumstances
- mindless repetition of short phrases
- emptying one's self of everything possible
- simply memorizing Scripture passages
- assuming an unusual position for spiritual illumination
- chanting
- detaching your mind from reality for short amounts of time

Meditating on God's Word *is*:
- bringing God into one's circumstances
- applying treasures from God's Word to daily life
- filling one's self with God's living, active, and effective Word
- more than just memorizing; it is taking God's Word into one's heart
- easy to do regardless of your location or physical position
- a powerful way to gain a deeper understanding of reality from God's perspective
- the avenue through which prosperity and success come, *"Do not let this Book of the Law depart from your mouth; meditate on it day and night, so that you may be careful to do everything written in it. Then you will be prosperous and successful"* (Joshua 1:8).

The Blessings of Meditation

Let's look at what David, a man after God's own heart (Acts 13:22), had to say about the value of meditating: *"Blessed is the man who does not walk in the counsel of the wicked or stand in the way of sinners or sit in the seat of mockers. But his delight is in the law of the LORD, and on his law he meditates day and night. He is like a tree planted by streams of water, which yields its fruit in season and whose leaf does not wither. Whatever he does prospers"* (Psalms 1:1-3).

Notice in the first verse that David talks about us walking, standing, and sitting. The important issue is in choosing *where* we walk, sit, and stand. We may choose to walk, sit, and/or stand with mockers, willful sinners, or in the counsel of the ungodly. However, we must also realize that these "locations" are not connected with a state of blessing.

Moving on to verse two, we see a person who sits, stands, and walks in the Word—a person who **meditates on the Word**. Then, in verse 3, we are told the rewards of meditating on the Word.

The person who meditates on the Word:
- has great stability—*like a tree planted by streams of water*
- has constant access to fresh supplies—*by streams of water*
- is a productive and fruitful person—*yields its fruit in season*
- understands godly timing—*in season*
- has life continually coursing throughout every area of his life—*whose leaf does not wither*
- prospers in whatever he does

To make it simple, a person who meditates on the Word has stability, fresh supply in God, is productive and fruitful, understands godly timing, virtually overflows with life, and is prosperous in whatever he does. The key to godly success is *meditating on God's Word!*

Fall in Love With His Word

Do you remember the first time you ever "fell in love"? Do you remember how you savored the other person's words, and let those words settle into your thinking? In a similar way, Jesus is waiting on you to give Him the opportunity to let His Word become the delight of your heart. In order to get the full benefit of His Word, we need to commit ourselves to letting it settle into us. It's hard for a love relationship with God to develop into anything of substance if we don't commit to listening, interacting, and esteeming His Word. Therefore, I want to challenge you to use *SOUL FOOD* as a means of growing in Christ. This book is designed to help you progress into a deeper and closer walk with God!

Let me also challenge you to provide God with the opportunity to reveal Himself to you by completing this devotional. If you approach Him in a nonchalant and casual way, do not expect to have a very deep relationship with Him. As in any relationship with depth, both parties must commit to that relationship. God has committed Himself to being close to you, and He awaits the walking out of your commitment to Him.

If you commit to meditate on some of the verses in Psalm 119, as you make your way through *SOUL FOOD*, you will come to know Christ in a more intimate way than you now know Him. I know this because it says in Isaiah 55:10-11: *"As the rain and the snow come down from heaven, and do not return to it without watering the earth and making it bud and flourish, so that it yields seed for the sower and bread for the eater,* **so is my word that goes out from my mouth: It will not return to me empty, but will accomplish what I desire and achieve the purpose for which I sent it."**

The Fruit of Commitment

The commitment that will reap the most fruit from this study is as follows:

#1 Commit to read each section carefully as part of your devotion time. First, take a day to read the introductory explanation for each letter, and then do one devotion daily thereafter.

#2 Commit to meditate (memorize, personalize, and visualize) certain verses of your choice. You might pick specific verses that speak directly to you, or select a complete section, or choose the first verse in each section, or you may ambitiously decide to meditate on every verse in Psalm 119!

#3 Commit to let God change you and mold you into His image, while He reveals Himself to you in greater depth.

The first item listed above is fairly self-explanatory. Meditating is something you will need to do as you can, utilizing free minutes throughout your day whenever possible. Realize from the outset that if you have a fairly demanding schedule, there may be times when you won't get a verse done for the day. Don't give up! There will be other days when you will be able to do a little more than a single verse. This is not an overwhelming nor unreasonable goal—particularly when we are seeking to let God change us and to develop greater intimacy with Him. The third point is also self-explanatory.

Don't be intimidated by these goals. My objective in this lesson is to encourage you to commit to finish what you start so that you will obtain a more absorbing walk with God.

The MVP's of Meditation

Now, let's look at the meaning of **meditate**. Meditation has three parts. If you ever played sports, you may have received an award called the **M.V.P.**— the Most Valuable Player. When it comes to the "game of life," there's no more valuable player on your team than the Word of God. The more you meditate on the Word, the greater impact it has on you. Meditating on the Word is truly your "Most Valuable Player"—your **M.V.P.**

The **M.V.P.** of meditating has three parts:
- **M** (memorize)
- **V** (visualize)
- **P** (personalize)

The first step in meditating on the Word is to *"memorize."* I find the easiest way to meditate is to begin my new verse at night, right before I go to bed. Then, in bed, I review my newly learned verse (even though it's usually not 100% perfect) a few times before I go to sleep. As I sleep, my brain is going over the new verse so that when I look at it in the morning, it "sticks to my ribs" much more readily.

Throughout my day, I work on my new verse and, generally, by the evening I know my verse for the day fairly well. Sometimes, I'll have a verse that's longer than usual, or I'll have a difficult time getting it. I don't let that frustrate me. I just keep chipping away at it, regardless of how slowly I progress. Ultimately I will get the verse memorized. The key is that I don't let myself get discouraged with my pace. I just keep plodding along, continuing to let the Word chip away at me.

Right now, I want to encourage you to begin working on a verse of your choice, regardless of where you are in your day. Be sure to focus particularly on it right before you go to bed.

Take a moment at this point to pray, asking Jesus to help you be a teachable student for the time you will spend in this book. Ask Him to help you hear His voice clearly and distinctly while you are meditating upon His Word.

As we talk about meditating on the Word, we need to realize that meditating is much more than simply memorizing, and consequently has more benefits than just learning for memory's sake. The goal of meditating on the Word is to let God's Word settle and take root in the deepest core of who we are, allowing it to conform us to Jesus' likeness!

While memorizing is important, merely memorizing is like deciding to eat an orange and peeling it without tasting its delicious fruit. In my opinion, simply memorizing God's Word without attempting to squeeze further life and application out of it is a tragedy. God's Word is meant to dig into us, take root and produce fruit through us. Simply memorizing the Word is like scattering seeds on concrete—they will not bear much fruit.

Visualize the Verse

The next part of meditating in our **M.V.P.** lineup is the *"V,"* which stands for *"visualizing."* When you visualize your verse, you put yourself into the verse and you see it happen—you put your verse into 3-D.

One time, some people were depending on me to do a lot of the details for their visit to Denver. As their expectations grew, I began developing a bad attitude about helping them. I wanted to have the right attitude but, as much as I tried, I just was not able to **make** myself have a godly attitude. I was frustrated.

At the time, I was meditating on I Peter 4:9, *"Offer hospitality to one another without grumbling."* As I began to meditate on this verse, I noticed that I no longer had to work to maintain the right attitude. It was as if someone had turned a switch on in me. Suddenly, it was the most natural thing for me *to want* to help my friends. Thank God for His life-changing Word!

Make It Personal

The *"P"* represents the word *"personalize."* When we talk about personalizing, we mean applying the verse and passage to oneself by actually using words that make the verse *personal.* Let me use an example. A friend once told me something very powerful. He said, "God can do through you what you cannot do." When I first heard the statement, it sounded nice. However, as I began to think about it and to personalize it, it became increasingly powerful. I examined the statement a few different ways to make it more personal.

First, I put myself into the statement: "God can do through **Sarah** what **she** cannot do." I thought about that for awhile, applying it to some seemingly impossible situations. Then I took another step, personalizing the statement a little more: "God can do through **me** what **I** cannot do."

Finally, I took this personalizing exercise a step further by looking upward to God and saying/thinking the statement: "**You** can do through **me** what **I** cannot do." Now, the statement is very real and invigorating to me!

Now you know the **M.V.P.s** of meditation: **Memorize, Visualize,** and **Personalize.** As you select some verses in Psalm 119, put the **M.V.P.s** to work. I suggest you keep a notebook or journal to record some of the rich revelation that the Holy Spirit gives as you put these verses in your heart through meditation. Remember, the goal of meditating on the Word is to let God's Word settle and take root in the deepest core of who you are, allowing it to conform you to Jesus' likeness!

Bibliography

Auch, Ron, *The Heart of the King*. Green Forest, Arkansas:
New Leaf Press, 1995.

Hirsch, Samson Raphael, *The Psalms, Volume II*. New York:
Philipp Feldheim, Inc., 1966.

Hickey, Marilyn, *Psalms Classic Library Edition*. Denver, Colorado:
Marilyn Hickey Ministries, 1997.

Mills, Dick and Michael, David, *Messiah and His Hebrew Alphabet*.
Orange, California: Dick Mills Ministries, 1996.

Novak, Al, *Hebrew Honey*, Houston, Texas:
J. Countryman Publishers, 1987.

Spurgeon, C. H., *The Treasury of David, Volume III*.
Peabody, Massachusetts: Hendrickson Publishers

Receive Jesus Christ as Lord and Savior of Your Life.

The Bible says, *"That if thou shalt confess with thy mouth the Lord Jesus, and shalt believe in thine heart that God raised him from the dead, thou shalt be saved. For with the heart man believeth unto righteousness; and with the mouth confession is made unto salvation"* (Romans 10:9,10).

To receive Jesus Christ as Lord and Savior of your life, sincerely pray this prayer from your heart:

Dear Jesus,

I believe that You died for me and that You rose again on the third day I confess to You that I am a sinner and that I need Your love and forgiveness. Come into my life, forgive my sins, and give me eternal life. I confess You now as my Lord. Thank You for my salvation!

Signed _____ Date _____

Please print.

Name Mr. & Mrs. / Mr. / Miss / Mrs. _____

Address _____

City _____ State _____ Zip _____

Phone (H) (   ) _____

Write to us.
We will send you information to help you with your new life in Christ.

Marilyn Hickey Ministries
P.O. Box 17340 • Denver, CO 80217 • 303-770-0400
www.mhmin.org

TOUCHING YOU WITH THE LOVE OF JESUS!

Marilyn Hickey PRAYER CENTER

When was the last time that you could say, "He touched me, right where I hurt"? No matter how serious the nature of your call, we're here to pray the Word and show you how to touch Jesus for real answers to real problems.

Call us and let's touch Jesus, together!

303-796-1333

Open 4 a.m.—4:30 p.m. Monday—Friday (MT).

WE CARE!

Prayer Request(s)

Let us join our faith with yours for your prayer needs. Fill out the coupon below and send to Marilyn Hickey Ministries, P.O. Box 17340, Denver, CO 80217.

Prayer Request(s) _____

_____

_____

_____

_____

_____

Mr. & Mrs.
Mr.   Please print.
Name Miss _____
     Mrs.

Address _____

City _____

State _____ Zip _____

Phone (H) (   ) _____

     (W) (   ) _____

If you want prayer immediately, call our Prayer Center at 303-796-1333, Monday-Friday, 4 a.m.—4:30 p.m. (MT).

BOOKS BY MARILYN HICKEY

A Cry for Miracles $7.95
Acts of the Holy Spirit $7.95
Angels All Around $7.95
Armageddon $4.95
Ask Marilyn $9.95
Be Healed $9.95
Bible Encounter Classic Edition $24.95
Blessing Journal $4.95
Book of Revelation Comic Book (The) $3.00
Break the Generation Curse $7.95
Break the Generation Curse –Part 2 .... $9.95
Building Blocks for Better Families $4.95
Daily Devotional $7.95
Dear Marilyn $7.95
Devils, Demons, and Deliverance $9.95
Divorce Is Not the Answer $7.95
Especially for Today's Woman $14.95
Freedom From Bondages $7.95
Gift-Wrapped Fruit $2.95
God's Covenant for Your Family $7.95
God's Rx for a Hurting Heart $4.95
Hebrew Honey $14.95
How to Be a Mature Christian $7.95
Know Your Ministry $4.95
Maximize Your Day . . . God's Way $7.95
Miracle Signs and Wonders $24.95
Names of God (The) $7.95
Nehemiah—Rebuilding the Broken Places in Your Life $7.95
No. 1 Key to Success—Meditation (The) $4.95
Proverbs Classic Library Edition $24.95
Release the Power of the Blood Covenant $4.95
Satan-Proof Your Home $7.95
Save the Family Promise Book $14.95
Signs in the Heavens $7.95
What Every Person Wants to Know About Prayer $4.95
When Only a Miracle Will Do $4.95
Your Miracle Source $4.95
Your Total Health Handbook—Body • Soul • Spirit $9.95

Prices are in U.S. dollars. If ordering in foreign currency, please calculate the current exchange rate.

For Your Information
Free Monthly Magazine

☐ Please send me your free monthly magazine,
   OUTPOURING (including daily devotionals, timely
   articles, and ministry updates)!

Tapes and Books

☐ Please send me Marilyn's latest product catalog.

Mr. & Mrs.   Please print.
Mr.
Miss
Name Mrs._____

Address _____

City _____

State _____ Zip _____

Phone (H) (   ) _____

    (W) (   ) _____

Mail to:
Marilyn Hickey Ministries
P.O. Box 17340
Denver, CO 80217
303-770-0400

WORD
to the
WORLD
COLLEGE

Explore your options and increase your knowledge of the Word at this unique college of higher learning for men and women of faith. Word to the World College offers **on-campus and correspondence courses** that give you the opportunity to learn from Marilyn Hickey and other great Bible scholars. WWC can help prepare you to be an effective minister of the gospel. Classes are open to both full- and part-time students.

For more information, complete the coupon below and send it to:

- -

Word to the World College
P.O. Box 17340
Denver, CO 80217
303-770-0400

Mr.
Mrs.   Please print.
Name Miss _____

Address_____

City _____ State _____ Zip _____

Phone (H) _____ (W) _____

Marilyn Hickey Ministries

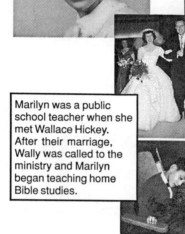

Marilyn was a public school teacher when she met Wallace Hickey. After their marriage, Wally was called to the ministry and Marilyn began teaching home Bible studies.

The vision of Marilyn Hickey Ministries is to "cover the earth with the Word" (Isaiah 11:9). For over 30 years Marilyn Hickey has dedicated herself to an anointed, unique, and distinguished ministry of reaching out to people—from all walks of life—who are hungry for God's Word and all that He has for them. Millions have witnessed and acclaimed the positive, personal impact she brings through fresh revelation knowledge that God has given her through His Word.

Marilyn has been the invited guest of government leaders and heads of state from many nations of the world. She is considered by many to be one of today's greatest ambassadors of God's Good News to this dark and hurting generation.

The more Marilyn follows God's will for her life, the more God uses her to bring refreshing, renewal, and revival to the Body of Christ throughout the world. As His obedient servant, Marilyn desires to follow Him all the days of her life.

Marilyn and Wally adopted their son Michael; through a fulfilled prophecy they had their daughter Sarah, who with her husband Reece, is now part of the ministry.

Marilyn founded her ministry "Life for Laymen" so that she could reach more people with her gift for practical Bible application.

Marilyn taught at Denver's "Happy Church" and hosted ministry conferences with husband Wally.

At a retreat in 1976, Marilyn realized she was called to "cover the earth with the Word."

The ministry staff in the early days helped Marilyn answer the mail that came in response to her first 15-minute radio show.

Soon Marilyn realized how many more people she could reach by going on television. She and Wally hosted many well known guests.

In Guatemala with former President Ephraim Rios-Mott

Marilyn has been the invited guest of government leaders and heads of state from many nations of the world.

In Venezuela with first lady Mrs. Perez

In Egypt with Mrs. Anwar Sadat

In Lebanon with Major Haddad

Marilyn ministers to guerillas in Honduras and brings food and clothing to the wives and children who are encamped with their husbands.

The popular Bible reading plan "Time With Him" began in 1978 and invited people to "read through the Bible with Marilyn." The monthly ministry magazine has since been renamed "Outpouring." It now includes a calendar of ministry events, timely articles, and featured product offers.

Through Word to the World College (formerly Marilyn Hickey Bible College), Marilyn is helping to equip men and women to take the gospel around the world.

Recently dorms were added to the campus facilities.

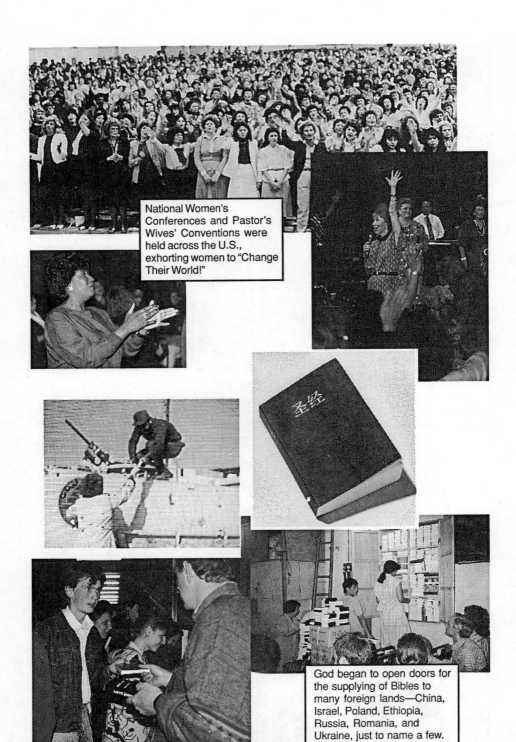

National Women's Conferences and Pastor's Wives' Conventions were held across the U.S., exhorting women to "Change Their World!"

God began to open doors for the supplying of Bibles to many foreign lands—China, Israel, Poland, Ethiopia, Russia, Romania, and Ukraine, just to name a few.

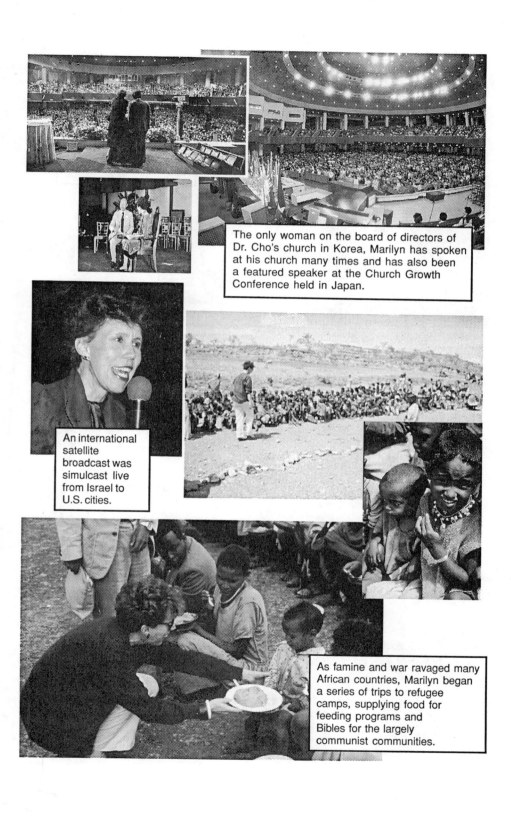

The only woman on the board of directors of Dr. Cho's church in Korea, Marilyn has spoken at his church many times and has also been a featured speaker at the Church Growth Conference held in Japan.

An international satellite broadcast was simulcast live from Israel to U.S. cities.

As famine and war ravaged many African countries, Marilyn began a series of trips to refugee camps, supplying food for feeding programs and Bibles for the largely communist communities.

The ministry expanded from its beginnings in a cardboard box, to the first International Ministry Center, built in 1985, to present headquarters located in Greenwood Village, Colorado.

FILL THE SHIP, a special project of the Marilyn Hickey Children's Fund, supplies food and Bibles to various Third World countries, such as Haiti, the Philippines, Ethiopia, Honduras, and El Salvador.

The prime time television special, "A Cry for Miracles," featured co-host Gavin MacLeod.

Over 1,500 ministry products help people in all areas of their life.

Marilyn Hickey's Prayer Center handles calls from all over the U.S.— ministering to those who need agreement in prayer.

Marilyn ministered in underground churches in Romania before any of the European communist countries were officially open.

Ministry and speaking engagement at a Women's Conference in Nigeria

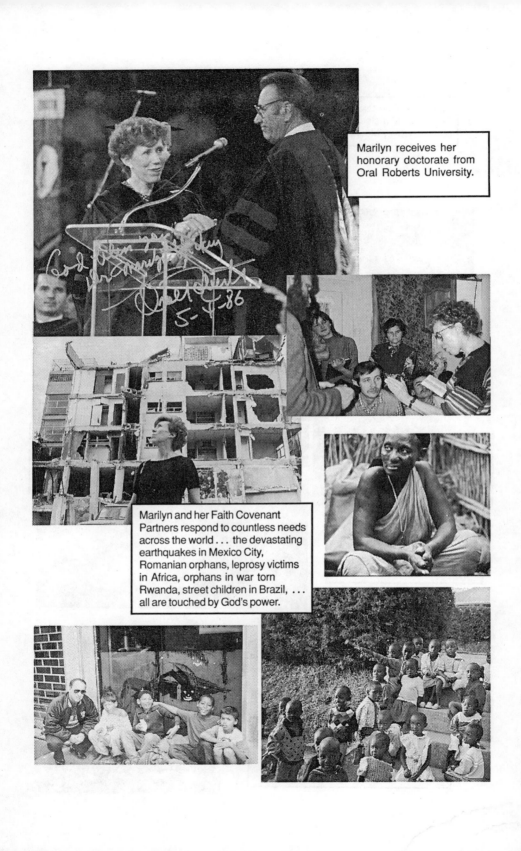

Marilyn receives her honorary doctorate from Oral Roberts University.

Marilyn and her Faith Covenant Partners respond to countless needs across the world . . . the devastating earthquakes in Mexico City, Romanian orphans, leprosy victims in Africa, orphans in war torn Rwanda, street children in Brazil, . . . all are touched by God's power.

Marilyn has been a guest several times on the 700 Club with host Pat Robertson.

Airlift Manila provided much needed food, Bibles, and personal supplies to the Philippines; MHM also raised funds to aid in the digging of water wells for those without clean drinking water.

Marilyn participates in a "devil-stomp" on prayer requests: thousands are received daily from friends and partners all over the world and are prayed over by Marilyn and the staff.

MHM supports Mission of Mercy in Calcutta, headed by Huldah Buntain. Marilyn has made several trips there.

Missions' trips to China are really close to Marilyn's and Sarah's hearts. Thousands of Bibles have been smuggled across the borders.

"Today With Marilyn" Bible teaching program is broadcast weekdays on TBN, BET, and several independent stations. The program is also seen overseas by millions through Christian Network TV, in Australia on Network 10, and in more than 80 other countries worldwide.

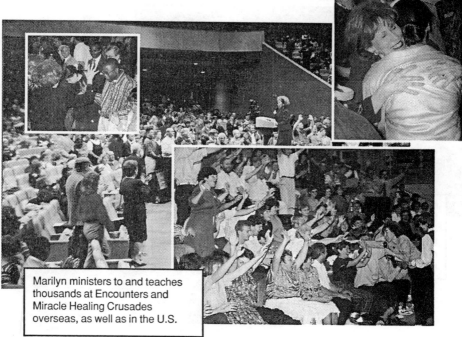

Marilyn ministers to and teaches thousands at Encounters and Miracle Healing Crusades overseas, as well as in the U.S.

Exciting ministry opportunities awaited Marilyn and her team of travelers in Ukraine and Russia, as the doors opened for the Gospel.

Victim of the nuclear power plant disaster in Chernobyl

Marilyn has held Bible Encounters in Malaysia and Singapore. While traveling through Hong Kong she ministered to Vietnamese in a refugee camp.

Ministry trips and cruises to places such as Indonesia, Russia, Greece, Ukraine, Turkey, and Israel offer short-term missions' opportunities to travel with Marilyn to exotic places.

Overseas offices have recently been set up in the United Kingdom, Australia, and South Africa. Marilyn also hosts yearly meetings, crusades, and missions' projects in those countries.

Crowds of up to 200,000 attended the open-air crusade in Bangalore, India.

In Islamabad, Pakistan, Marilyn held Ministry Training Schools. Total crusade attendance was estimated at 70,000.

Eritrea and Sudan—Ministry Training Schools, nightly crusades and Madagascar crusade with Sarah and Marilyn ministering